Journeys of Discovery: A Design for Expansive Learning

Arthur K. Ellis and Richard D. Scheuerman

J.A. & Kathryn Albertson
CENTER FOR EDUCATIONAL
EXCELLENCE

To Shelly,
With warmest personal
regards to a collegue and
friend.
Sincerely,
[signature]
29·X·01

J.A. & Kathryn Albertson Foundation
Center for Educational Excellence
501 Baybrook Court
Boise, Idaho 70002

Mountain Light Homepage: mountainlightschool.com

For information about Mountain Light's Journeys of Discovery curriculum
materials, write: DEMCO, Inc., P. O. Box 7488, Madison, Wisconsin 53707-7488
www.demco.com

ISBN: 0-9705986-0-2

For Arden Johnson,
who first suggested we take the journey,

and for Karl, Jared, Jason, and Nicholas,
who did.

Acknowledgements

We would like to thank the following individuals and institutions for offering their partnership, expertise, and encouragement in the development of the Journeys of Discovery experience and in the preparation of this book.

Sharon Jarvis, Trudy Anderson	*J.A. & Kathryn Albertson Foundation*
Wayne Rush, Kathleen Elliott	*Boise, Idaho*
Harriet Bullitt	*Bullitt Foundation, Seattle, Washington*
Carla Nuxoll, Lynn Simmons	*U.S. Department of Education*
Larry McLure, Richard Melo	*Northwest Regional Educational Laboratory, Portland, Oregon*
Bob Subota	*Office of the Idaho State Superintendent of Public Instruction, Boise, Idaho*
Gayle Pauley, Tom Hulst	*Office of the Washington State Superintendent of Public Instruction, Olympia, Washington*
Gary Schneidmiller	*Post Falls, Idaho*
John Rutter	*National Geographic Society, Washington, D.C.*
Ed Muir, Jeff Glover	*DEMCO, Madison, Wisconsin*
Cherie Major, Frank Powers	*University of Idaho, Moscow*
James Beane, Barbara Broadhagen	*National Louis University, Madison, Wisconsin*
David Palumbo, Suzanne Rhodes	*Human Code, Austin, Texas*
Michael and Lynda Sheets	*ARO Designs, Spokane, WA*

Mountain Light School Consortium

Tim McCarthy, Dennis Bolz, Bernadette Griffith, Fred Morrison, Keith Merritt, Mark Johnson, Suzanne Schmick, Sue Lynch, Tim Nootenboom, Glenn Johnson, Carol Jeffries, Tom Alsbury, Mike Franza, Ed Tuggle, Randy Bloom, Mark Mansell

Mountain Light Development Team

Richard Johnson, Lois Scheuerman, James LeGette, Diane Yettick, Arden Johnson, Julie Lust, Jo Petersen, Sandy Siler, Nona Hengen, Bill Black, Don Scheuerman, Karl Scheuerman, Jason Siler, Nicholas Siler, Jared Wolfe

Mountain Light International Advisory Board

Michael Bottery, University of Hull, Leeds, England; Chen Cunfu, Zhejiang University, Hangzhou, China; Francis Luttikhuizen, University of Barcelona, Spain; Ernest Grigorian, Russian Academy of Pedagogical Sciences, Moscow, Russia

Foreword

Over four decades advocates for reform in education have pressed to make schools more responsive to the young adolescents who attend them. Their efforts have not been without success, for there is a growing body of evidence that where the educational reform platform has been taken seriously, students and teachers have benefited in significant ways. Most reform efforts, though, have emphasized the need for more positive climate and flexible structures, while less attention has been paid to the planned curriculum. Indeed, it is hard to imagine that this movement would reach it largest potential without serious work on the curriculum. After all, the curriculum in many ways defines the day-to-day life of students and teachers and mediates relationships among them.

Yet the curriculum in far too many of our schools is little changed from the "dull and lifeless" fare journalist Charles Silberman found in junior high schools three decades ago or the lackluster one described in the national "shadow studies" carried out by John Lounsbury and his collegues during the 1970's and 80's. It is a curriculum that consists mainly of a dizzying array of disconnected and incoherent facts and skills that engage neither the intellect nor the imagination of young adolescents. Its challenge lies mostly in perseverance. What might be done about this situation? To begin with, we might well think about how to enliven the content of the curriculum, give it more depth, and organize it in ways that pique the innate curiosity that all young people have. This is what Richard Scheuerman and Arthur Ellis have done with the Journeys of Discovery curriculum.

Teachers who are looking for ways of moving beyond the recitation of dull facts within a fragmented, separate subject curriculum will find much to ponder and use within this study. The opening sections offer a well-constructed and compelling case for thinking about knowledge in terms of discovery rather than accumulation. Moreover, the authors argue eloquently for correlating and integrating knowledge in engaging contexts rather than parceling it out in single subject doses, thus giving knowledge more rather than less integrity for young adolescents. Thereafter, they provide us with a series of thematic units that are organized around historical "journeys of discovery." Each contains a wide variety of suggestions for activities that are meant to bring these episodes to life, and to encourage exploration and discovery through projects of many kinds.

At a time when so many educators and politicians seem to be defining curriculum improvement as longer lists of disconnected and disengaging facts and skills to be "mastered," it is heartening to encounter a work in which both knowledge and young people are treated more respectfully. Indeed, if there is one lesson to take away from the Journeys of Discovery, it would be this: a curriculum may be both academically challenging and intellectually engaging, both content-rich and project-centered. It would be helpful if more of our thinking about school curriculum would have such direction.

Dr. James A. Beane
National Louis University
Madison, Wisconsin

Contents

Introduction

The Mountain Light School
Fall, 1920

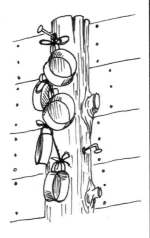

Nestled alongside a steep hillside in the heart of Idaho and Washington's rolling Palouse Country rests the remains of a one-room country schoolhouse. For several decades after the turn of the nineteenth century, the Mountain Light School served as a vibrant rural community center of learning that frequently brought area families together for recreation, entertainment, and fellowship. A sepia photograph taken in the fall of 1920 evokes memories of a proud structure built by local hands appearing eager for a new term to begin. Visible even today are the warm orange-brown exterior walls with cream colored trim that rest upon a high foundation built to withstand any flash flood. In a design typical of the era, the structure was crowned with a distinctive cupola of concave sides suggesting an Oriental influence incongruous with the surrounding grainlands. Yet the experiences shared by those who came for miles around to ascend its nine wooden steps would one day securely direct their paths both east and west.

Few artifacts remain that bear witness to the purposes for which the building was raised other than a half-dozen tin cups suspended together by heavy string on a post. A nearby pail held water to refresh the pupils who shared these cups throughout the day. They were carefully washed by students who often remained after hours to assist the teacher. In 1920 Miss Vera Longwell arrived from Kansas to begin a distinguished teaching career, boarding with a neighboring farm family which included six of her pupils. Miss Longwell would not permit less dutiful work after class than during lessons but her kindly demeanor is recalled with fondness by her former students as is the sense of wonder, accomplishment, and pride—in that order—that she so skillfully fostered.

Reminiscing at a half-century's distance, Miss Longwell's pupils are quick to note methods that distinctly shaped their learning: cross-age groupings in which the younger assisted the older as often as not, studying the classics and primary source materials followed by public presentations of written and dramatic works. The curriculum included thematic units of study throughout the year with implicit contemporary relevance both to the locale and to the greater world. Tales of Robin Hood and Sherwood Forest occasioned trips to an anonymous grove of willow and hawthorne trees where botany easily became a topic of inquiry. *Saturday Evening Post* reviews of the Boston Symphony's 1920 premier of "The Pleasure Dome of Kublai Khan" led naturally to stories of Marco Polo, the poetry of Samuel Taylor Coleridge ("In Xanadu did Kublai Khan..."), and news of Babe Ruth's trade that year from Boston to the Yankees for $125,000. That remarkable sum, in turn, offered grist for a lesson in mathematics. Before anyone realized how much time and work had passed, recess break was announced and students regrouped outside to claim one of two swings or play run-sheep-run.

A photograph taken at the end of the school year shows Miss Longwell surrounded by a sea of faces, young and old alike, as parents and their children gathered in late spring for a festive afternoon of picnicking, declamations, and group performance. The young people seem both excited over the prospect of summer vacation and confident that the security of home, school, and community promised a hopeful future. Those in attendance had reason to feel secure and confident. From those pictured and others in the vicinity, this small community would contribute a generation of successful parents, citizens, and workers in business, agriculture, and industry. Graduates included a Marine general, state governor, and the nation's first woman ophthalmologist. When asked the nature of her inspiration for attainment, one former Mountain Light pupil replied, "We were taught to live responsibly as a school family and express our natural curiosity to discover the world around us."

We have found the metaphor of learning as discovery to be a powerful means to reinvent education for a new era. This orientation empowers students to be more responsible for their learn-

"Many so-called 'innovations' being championed today were born of necessity long ago in the rural schoolhouse. Cooperative learning, multigrade classrooms, intimate links between school and community, interdisciplinary studies, peer tutoring, block scheduling, the community as the focus of study, older students teaching younger ones, sitebased management, and close relationships between teachers and students all characterize these school practices."

The Condition of American Education, *U.S. Department of Education (1998)*

ing and chart a course for instructional destinies over which they can assert greater choice. Expansive learning through instructional technology is possible today in ways that were beyond comprehension when the cupola was built on the Mountain Light country school. The solid foundation of that place's nurtured sense of wonder, belonging, and community remain the primal attributes in the sacred task of stewarding young minds for enduring emotional and intellectual wellbeing. But learning as discovery, using technology to open vast new realms of inquiry and community-building, involves learning environments that cannot be confined to conventional textbooks and worksheets, though these may serve as useful resources. From virtually any place in the world today, information technology makes it possible to hear the music of the Boston Symphony, information on the latest trades in professional baseball or the stock market, and online visits to places from Sherwood Forest to Mars and beyond. The pedagogical challenge becomes one of managing the rapidly expanding knowledge base in this new era of discovery, fostering an appreciation for its wise use, and ensuring that our efforts build strong academic abilities needed by young people to successfully chart a course for their future. The Journeys of Discovery curriculum and approach to expansive learning represent such an organizing system.

Few other endeavors or themes invite the kinds of dynamic associations for challenging curriculum as discovery and exploration. Students' "natural curiosity" of the world evidenced at the Mountain Light school remains a powerful impetus to build proficiencies in the knowledge and skills deemed essential to a twenty-first century comprehensive education. As William H. Goetzmann has observed, "Exploration is a unique process that has enabled mankind to know and understand.... *[It] represents the process of learning in its most expansive form.*" For these reasons and in order to provide instructional experiences that combine for reinforcement rather than separate essential learning tasks, the Journeys of Discovery lessons open with an authentic "travelogue reading" taken from a primary resource associated with the Journey under study. These readings themselves constitute a vital part of our diverse cultural heritage and are outstanding literary selections in their own right. Moreover, the Journeys series is founded on the very basic assumption that students and teachers desire to search for ideas and insights—that we are all explorers at heart! This is not pedagogical näiveté for, as Harvard scientist Edward Wilson points out, more remains yet to be discovered in our own terrestial realm and beyond than has been since the dawn of time.

Geography represents a pivotal link in the Journeys curriculum as geography's essence is one of both human and physical dimensions. H. J. MacKinder writes that geography "postulates both scientific and human knowledge. If our aim is to give unity to the outlook of our pupils, and to stop that pigeon-holing of subjects in their minds which has prevailed in the past, then geography is admirably fitted as a correlating medium." The epic exploration accounts featured in the Journeys of Discovery take learners directly to original journals, letters, and related records, freeing the imagination and allowing the quest for quality interdisciplinary learning to take place. Furthermore, readings attempt to draw attention to the valuable contributions made in the annals of epic discovery by teenagers—Sakakawea and George Shannon with Lewis & Clark, naturalist George Forster on board Captain Cook's bark *Resolution,* and Marco Polo himself, as well as such women as Elizabeth I, Eleanor of Aquitaine, and Jessie Frémont. Journeys of Discovery invite participants to become scientists, historians, mathematicians, artists, and builders in an attempt to transform learning into the active construction of lasting ideas and values, revealed with contemporary relevance.

The oral reading and discussing of these brief selections is the instructional opening to the day's events and from them emerge myriad topics identified by students and prominently posted for the research and presentation choices that will constitute a significant part of that week's instructional agenda. ("A World of Illustrated Journaling Possibilities" outlines these options for students.) With "hands-on" activities derived from each of the daily readings, an intellectual renaissance becomes possible.

William Clark in receipt of Lewis' June, 1803 letter inviting him to participate in the expedition's "fatigues, dangers, and honors."

On Tuesday *we made it to Barcelona, one of Spain s major Mediterranean seaports. The Museum of Modern Art was very interesting and had a special exhibit of paintings by Salvador Dali. A photograph of this remarkable artist with trademark upturned mustache showed him standing next to one of the works that was on display. Viewing* Day at the Beach *was like entering a dream. Images of round bodies floated through the air like clouds of dull color. I liked it very much. On the way back to the Hotel Pamplona, Rocky tried to break away from the leash as he kept wanting to dart into shops in which freshly killed chickens and hams hung like purses at Nordstrom. This part of Barcelona is called the Rambla and was our favorite place because of all the open-air markets. I saw a poster advertising the local Fiera, or annual fair, and I remembered that Juan, the guide we met back at the hotel, said the fair would be the best place to see the fantastic folk artists who descend from Pyrennes each year to show their wares.*

Andrew Reinertsen, 6th grade, enroute with The Exploits of Columbus and the Conquistadors: New World Journeys of Discovery.

Dale Stolmeier, 7th grade

Illustrated Journaling Presentations

Options for Writing

Writing responses to Journeys travelogue experiences may take many forms. Since writing is the best indicator of thought and can be expressed in so many ways, try different approaches that give you opportunities to better develop your own knowledge and share your understandings with others. Remember to always date each writing response.

Journals   Compose a paragraph to continue the travel journal as you follow a great explorer s route.

Editorials   Write an article expressing your opinion on a topic related to the reading.

Poetry   Compose a free verse or rhyme poem about a place or topic under study.

News Stories   Pretend you are a reporter on the scene doing a story for the local newspaper.

Play Scripts   Create a script for a scene with parts for two to four characters.

Letters   Write a friendly letter to someone describing a discovery experience or a business letter expressing your ideas on a topic of interest or concern to a newspaper editor, public official, or organization.

Myth   Compose a myth explaining the distinguishing characteristics of an interesting animal, the shape of a star pattern, or other natural phenomenon.

Short Story   Write a story about a real or imagined incident or individual encountered in your study with attention to setting and characterization.

Interviews   Develop a script for an interview between a host and famous guest or someone in a career of your personal interest.

Resource Reviews   Describe and summarize a related magazine article, web site, or musical selection.

Ideas for Illustrating

Drawing   Create an image of something real or imagined associated with a topic under study. Start by being bold in your expression without concern about being exact. Gradually adjust and add details to produce a finished work.

Maps   Carefully draw and label a map showing a region under study. You may illuminate it with illustrations depicting places, people, flora, and fauna.

Field Sketch   Look carefully and sketch the intricate structure of a leaf, flower, insect, animal, or other natural object. Depict the special characteristics that distinguish it from other species.

Diagram   Show and label the cross-section of a structure, vehicle, ship, or other object; depict the main components of an idea, machine, or science project; create a top view of a building or place of significance to you.

Graph   Create a circle, bar, or line graph to show interesting statistical information like popular choices among classmates, temperature ranges in favorite places, etc.

Calligraphy   Use a style of formal lettering like Italic to express your thoughts in an interesting arrangement or to label a map or diagram.

Chart/Table   Arrange images of persons, animals, plants, or other objects to compare individuals, groups, or to display information in an interesting way.

Border Design   Think of an object or image past or present that can be carefully drawn and colored to enhance a page of your poetry or other writing.

Diorama/Model   Carefully construct a scale model of an object, place, or structure under study using simple materials like hardboard and glue.

Posters   Prepare a poster that captures the main idea or action of an event, book, movie, or other learning experience.

Timeline   Create a timeline that accurately shows the sequence of important events under study with illustrations of persons and places in the chronology, or that were in other parts of the world at the same time.

Ways for Presenting

Reading   Share orally a journal entry, editorial, or other original selection related to a place or time being studied.

Drama   Present a scene from a play as a readers theatre or performance with simple props.

Puppet Shows   Fashion cardboard characters and compose dialogue for a story or scene.

Television Programs   Present a brief show featuring an outdoor or museum tour, a cooking program, or some other aspect of a foreign culture.

Time Travel News: Go back in time for the evening news and present highlights of the city, nation, and world.

Suggested Rubric to Evaluate Student Journaling

(Levels within each category indicate beginning, developing and extending.)

Research   *Standard reference works and text materials used as directed (B).*

A variety of printed and electronic resources consulted to gain new knowledge (D).

A wide range of resources, experts, and primary source materials used independently (E).

Concept   *Expresses an idea in a complete sentence (B).*

Paragraphs develop main ideas; further details needed (D).

Content remains focused with effective paragraph transitions (E).

Style   *Vocabulary and sentences need variety and to reflect personal interest (B).*

New terms and expressions; ideas reflect personal involvement (D).

Original expressions and vivid descriptive language unique to author (E).

Conventions   *Capitalization, punctuation, and spelling often need correction (B).*

Occasional misspelled words and grammatical errors interfere with presentation (D).

Text flows without distraction from spelling and grammatical errors (E).

Illustrations   *Illustrations are attempted but representations are disorganized or unclear (B).*

Representation of new learnings and observations are clearly and variously shown (D).

A variety of illustrations are presented with understanding of line, form, and shading (E).

Delivery   *Voice projection and eye contact needed to effectively communicate (B).*

Projection and presence sufficient to inform listeners (D).

Effectively appeals to audience through voice, presence, and enthusiasm (E).

Revision   *Proofreading and suggestions to improve not evident in final draft (B).*

Peer evaluation and suggestions incorporated into final draft (D).

Contributes to peer evaluation and applies relevant comments (E).

Marco Polo in Kublai Khan's winter palace at Khanbalic.

The activities, whether experiments, drama, or reports, are the basis of intellectual engagement. Because writing is among the most important expressions of student thought for purposes of evaluation, students are encouraged to follow the example of great explorers by journalizing each week throughout the year. Entries based on topics identified through travelogue readings, freely determined or as assigned, provide an enriching record of student learning. Through literary engagements of their own design, students can develop writing skills in accordance with quality writing trait models while compiling unique portfolios of observations and discoveries along their own learning journeys. In addition to illustrated journal entries, students are free to offer editorials, poems, play scripts, interviews, and article and website reviews. When asked the inevitable question about "how much" constitutes an acceptable written contribution, one teacher pointed out to her students that James Cook wrote over one million words in the journals of his Pacific voyages without ever being required to do so. Of course the Earl of Sandwich was not expected to read and evaluate the quality of Cook's prose as teachers must.

In what may constitute the most extensive field trip ever undertaken by an adolescent, Marco Polo's travels across Asia in the thirteenth century demanded the development of knowledge and skills essential for success and survival. Stories of peoples and places so vividly described in his *Travels* reveal a mind challenged to read critically, communicate clearly, appreciate foreign cultures, and problem-solve. Whether determining directions by stars while traversing Central Asian deserts or presenting diplomatic reports at the court of the Kublai Khan, Marco's life of exploration exemplified learning on a grand scale. Students in a seventh grade class enroute with Marco Polo across northern India and Pakistan (travelogue reading 3.3: "A Region So Lofty") identified the following topics for investigation: mountain climbing, Buddhism, bighorn sheep, nuclear proliferation, *Mission Impossible 2,* Mt. Everest, predicting the future, and cobras. Students were free to work alone or in pairs to research these topics for presentations later during the week but were also required to complete a series of parallel Journeys sourcebook subject-area assignments, including an Arabian Nights story set in Central Asia, a mathematics lesson on mountain elevations, science activities related to medieval Asian astronomy, and an art project on Pakistani architecture. Similarly, travelogue selections from the journals of Lewis & Clark are correlated to significant writings and other records of prominent contemporaries who were deeply influenced by the Corps of Discovery's accomplishments: government reports of Thomas Jefferson, short stories by Washington Irving, the scientific contributions of John James Audubon, and the art of George Catlin.

The Journeys approach is relevant to learning in any place and at any age. The three-month curriculum travelogue and sourcebook modules are presently developed and arranged to correspond to themes typically taught at the intermediate and middle grades, and to knowledge and skills specified for those levels in the national content standards. Thus *The Travels of Marco Polo and Ibn Battuta: Asian and African Journeys of Discovery* relates well to seventh grade curriculum in many schools while *The Expeditions of Lewis & Clark and Zebulon Pike: North American Journeys of Discovery* may be more relevant for eighth graders. Others include *Eleanor of Aquitaine and the Crusade of the Kings: A Medieval Journey of Discovery,* and in progress, *The Exploits of Columbus and the Conquistadors: New World Journeys of Discovery* and *The Explorations of James Cook and Alexander Mackenzie: Pacific Rim Journeys of Discovery.*

Twelve Journeys are envisioned to complete the core series. Daily readings serve as touchstones for innumerable natural connections to period and regional literature readings, science units, art projects, and myriad field trip, cooperative learning, and electronic media activities. Students and teachers travel together across the forty-five travelogue selections in each module reflecting itineraries that in reality often took years to complete. Journeys team teachers should be allowed the instructional freedom to take sidetrips of serendipity and special interest much like Lewis's sojourn apart from the main party across western Montana. Perhaps a math unit on ratios and percents extends a week

"In recent years several reviews of research have been developed regarding the effects non-subject school curriculum designs have on student learning. This research has indicated that young people do better on measures on academic achievement as the curriculum moves beyond the separate subject approach in the direction of interdisciplinary and integration."

Handbook of Research on Teaching *(2000)*

beyond Clark's discourse on his St. Louis population census examined in social studies. The Journeys pedagogical expedition is sometimes strung out along the trail but staff can regroup with weekly faculty "camp meetings."

Sidebars on the left side of pages in this book's chapters contain brief selections from Journey travelogue readings while right sides and alternating lower page margins feature illustrations and a variety of writing forms by students in response to them. Student writing reflects a full range of achievement levels and comes from individuals with significant special needs to the highly capable. Samples have been drawn from a number of Journeys schools to illustrate experiences undertaken in urban, suburban, and rural settings. The examples demonstrate that for purposes of expansive learning, young people and mentoring adults can come together through learning and communication technologies to form communities that both transcend and celebrate the unique qualities of any school profile or region and culture.

The advance of civilizations is related to the expansion of the knowledge base and conditioned with the exercise of private and public virtue. The Journeys of Discovery curriculum seeks through direct instruction and independent research to propel students into contemplation of humanity's past experiences and consideration of future possibilities. Posing such questions is a fundamental aspect of progress. Relevant to this enterprise is the designation of "Leading Questions of Discovery" to remind learners of this imperative for quality classroom discussion, presentation, and writing lest in the words of T. S. Eliot, we "have the experience but miss the meaning." Placing these leading questions before students can elevate levels of understanding whether considering nomadic cultures and Asian literature or Byzantine mosaics and the periodic table. A modified taxonomy of understanding offers sample questions about subject area facts and skills, comprehension questions that relate knowledge to experiences and concepts that pervade the disciplines, and evaluation questions that involve judgements. Is this useful? Is this beautiful? Is this meaningful? Is this right? These are the ultimate questions with which we want

"The Journeys of Discovery curriculum seeks through direct instruction and independent research to propel learners into contemplation of humanity's past experiences and consideration of future possibilities."

students to grapple, and the Journeys of Discovery curriculum offers opportunity to do so as the whole of human experience across Time and Space is presented in a natural flow devoid of contrived connections and artificial separations.

Students are challenged to be lifelong learners and master basic skills by becoming aquainted with the achievements and character of such persons as Herodotus, Eleanor of Aquitaine, Saladin, Marco Polo, and Thomas Jefferson. These individuals and others like them were mindful that exploration and new knowledge should be used to benefit the next generation. Adolescence has ever been a time to test limits and question assumptions but young people nevertheless seek secure relationships and something in which to believe. A quality educational experience, therefore, ought to inspire through time-honored practices like storytelling, and through using new technologies to promote greater knowledge and skill development, virtue, and public service. The dramatic stories featured in the Journeys of Discovery curriculum represent a means to equip students in these ways through active experiences with cultural heritage. Furthermore, their participation aims to prepare them to face an array of complex environmental and social dilemmas while contributing to humankind's grasp of space, microworlds, and other frontiers that still await discovery and exploration.

Eleanor of Aquitaine, Henry of England, and Richard the Lionheart at Winchester Castle.

I

The Knowledge Explosion

Sidebars:
The Annals of Herodotus, Alexander and Pliny

The year 1859 was by all accounts a remarkable year set in a remarkable decade. It was especially significant in the annals of education and discovery. Charles Darwin's epic work *On the Origin of Species* was published in London, shaking the very foundations of the long-standing perception of a more static world and laying the groundwork for a new-found sense of priority of science as a school subject. From the deserts of Egypt the world learned that the oldest complete New Testament, the *Codex Sinaiticus*, had been found in an ancient monastery at the foot of Mt. Sinai. In the United States, John Dewey, whose long and productive career as a philosopher of education served to restructure the framework of the educational debate, was born—the same year that Horace Mann, the Father of American Education, died. And it was in 1859 that the English philosopher Herbert Spencer published his celebrated essay titled, "What Knowledge Is of Most Worth?"

In America, storm clouds gathered on the eve of the War between the States, and a fledgling political party that called itself the Republicans nominated as its presidential candidate in the coming year's election a little-known country lawyer named Abraham Lincoln. This was also the decade in which President Millard Fillmore dispatched Commodore Perry and the Great White Fleet to Japan, marking America's initial attempts to become a player on the world stage. The country's Centenary had yet to be celebrated, but already the battle for the common school had been won through the efforts of Mann in Massachusetts, Henry Barnard in Rhode Island, and other champions of the idea of compulsory, tax-supported schools for all boys and girls. In Mann's words, this was a birthright, and such thinking put the United States in the world forefront of free education for all.

But let us return to Herbert Spencer, the title of whose essay posed perhaps the most incisive question ever asked about education. When Spencer raised the question of what knowledge is of the most worth, he cast the debate in sharp relief. Answering the question would require thinking through the priorities of curriculum. Spencer had thrown down the gauntlet. Did certain school subjects deserve high priority simply because they had established themselves on the basis of long-standing tradition, or should there be a fundamental re-examination of the canon?

Spencer posed the question because he realized that the nations of Western Europe and North America were undergoing a great transformation out of which a new world would emerge. The first great transformation, the one that took human beings from hunting and gathering, slash and burn, and living a wandering, food-searching existence, to a more sedentary existence based on planting, tending, and harvesting crops, had taken centuries to accomplish. But it yielded a fruitful harvest in more ways than one. It had led to the design of cities, to the establishment of laws, to new forms of economics including mercantilism and the first lights of capitalism. And ultimately it led to schools, churches, libraries, museums, youth organizations, and other formal institutions of education.

Now, Spencer realized, the agricultural transformation was being superseded by a new transformation fueled by the Industrial Revolution. Thomas Jefferson's idealized sense of a nation of yeoman farmers was disappearing at a rapidly accelerating pace as people began to move off the land and into the cities in order to work in factories. This transformation, unlike its predecessor, was to be accomplished not in centuries but in about one hundred years.

The marriage between science and technology created new knowledge structures, both theoretical and applied. The work done in laboratories, experimental stations, and even in woodsheds and carriage barns was, in fact, creating an emergent educational tradition with origins dating back to the Renaissance and now rapidly accelerating. This was not so much the intent as it

Journeys
Poem

"Eratosthenes said to
his friend,
'I have a theory about
our earth,
And how it might be
measured.'
But his friend just
laughed,
So he gave him a
yardstick
To put into the
ground—
Exactly 12 noon was
the time.
In his town of
Cyrene,
Eratosthenes did the
same.
He hoped his friend in
Alexandria
Didn't think it was a
game...."

Katie Corder,
6th grade

HERODOTUS

"The Caspian is a separate sea, not joined to the other. The one on which the Greeks navigate and all that lies beyond the Pillars of Hercules, called the Atlantic, and the Red Sea are parts of the same sea; but the Caspian is all by itself. Along the western side of this sea is the Caucasus, of all the mountain ranges the greatest and loftiest, and in it dwell many peoples of diverse races."

Herodotus

was a by-product. In the most literal sense, a qualitatively different knowledge explosion was occurring—one fueled by science and technology—and it was finding its way into textbooks and school laboratories, challenging the academic hegemony of the seven liberal arts and their school-based derivatives. This was the intellectual matrix in which Spencer wrote his essay.

Spencer answered his own question by stating that the knowledge that is of most worth is the knowledge that contributes most to our survival—in other words, those activities that minister directly to self-preservation. Following this logic, he concluded that a knowledge of science is the "most useful for preparation for life," and it therefore must be included in the school curriculum. His powerful essay changed dramatically the purpose of education in the minds of many, away from an emphasis on the liberal arts and the idea of school as a place for the leisurely pursuit of ancient truths by a select few, toward an emphasis on more pragmatic social efficiency and life-adjustment goals for all.

An examination of the school curriculum prior to this decade and in the decades that followed shows a clear shift away from an emphasis on courses such as Greek and Latin and a new emphasis on such subjects as biology, modern languages, chemistry, and physics. The staying power of the rhetorical curriculum, with its

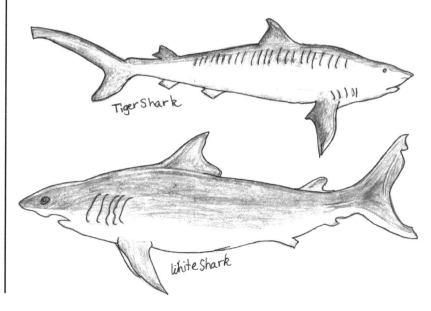

Tiger Shark

White Shark

emphasis on texts and authors, was not to be underestimated, however. Although the hard sciences found their way into the curriculum, they were, more often than not, textbook-based rather than investigatory in nature, and so a kind of compromise was made between the new content and the old delivery system.

This watershed in the history of school curriculum led to a whole variety of organizational, methodological, and curricular changes that are beyond the scope of this discussion. But more than anything else, it was the rapid expansion of the knowledge base that was forcing schools to change or be rendered irrelevant. So pervasive was the new knowledge based on science that it brought in its wake a new way of thinking about such traditional courses as history and the consequent emergence of new fields within the framework of something called social science. Thus "social science" as an analog of natural science.

However much one might challenge the pragmatic idea that the school experience should be one of social efficiency and life adjustment as opposed to the more classical idea of school as something reflective, leisurely, and purposefully set apart from the immediacies of real world demands, there was no denying the geometric expansion of knowledge itself beginning with this era. The sense of how to select that knowledge within curricular parameters continues to vex us to this day.

Journeys
Play
Script

Jacob: You know we're going to need scuba gear to find this place.
Josh: Sharks live in these waters so be careful.
Josh: Some archaeologists believe Atlantis was actually the Mediterranean island of Thera and that a volcano erupted there in 1500 B.C. and destroyed the place.
Richard: If we can't find it there I say we try the Canary Islands because some experts think it was an island that sunk near there.
Jacob: Hey, this detector is picking up something....

Jacob Sitton,
6th grade

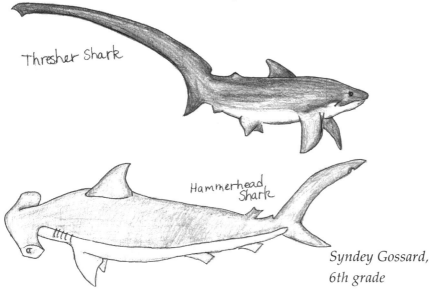

Thresher Shark

Hammerhead Shark

Syndey Gossard,
6th grade

ALEXANDER

The Knowledge Explosion

If one were to consider the expansion of the knowledge base, limiting such consideration only to the print medium, then it is possible to imagine a world of text copious enough to cover the earth to a depth of an inch by the decade of 1850. This would include all the printed material ever made from time immemorial—especially since the 15th century invention of the printing press. But as scholars such as Spencer understood, this was merely the beginning. In fact, in the space of one hundred years, from 1850-1950, the amount of printed material *doubled* to a depth of two inches. Imagine the difficulty of knowing what to leave in and what to leave out of the curriculum!

By 1950, the expansion of knowledge had taken on geometric dimensions, and in the space of time from 1950-1990 the amount of printed material increased to a depth of 36 inches. Only the naive and the unaware could surely suggest that it were possible to contain the needed curricular learning employing a traditional concept of knowledge. The unprecedented explosion of knowledge as presented in this metaphor includes, as you recall, only the *print* medium. The expansion of knowledge into electronic audio and visual forms further complicates the matter. In spite of this, there are teachers who are still devoted to coverage.

Alexander's Crown

As if the expansion of the amount of knowledge weren't a sufficiently complex matter itself, take a moment to consider the related issue of access to knowledge. In brief, access to knowledge has become greatly decentralized in our time. The former curators of the canon—the schools, libraries, and institutes—no longer possess the leverage and control they once enjoyed.

A generation ago the school and the town library were the central repositories of text knowledge. Texts were housed, controlled, and selectively distributed by the officials of these two educational institutions, the former limited to the young and based on a sequential set of age-graded teaching and learning experiences, and the latter available to all who could freely choose (from the texts available) a more random, uncredentialed course of learning. This is not to say that learning was limited solely to texts (film, theatre, radio, television, and travel have certainly been available for some time) or that text material itself could not be found in other places such as the corner drugstore, the occasional bookstore, the newspaper stand, and in privately owned collections. But texts were certainly the dominant player that defined and circumscribed the curriculum—as well as most random, vicarious access via the printed page to other times, places, and ideas.

To limit the knowledge explosion to paper text is to miss the point of much of what has happened with the development and

"When we decided to sign on for the expedition with Ulysses, I had no idea what was in store for us. My first hint that something was wrong happened soon after we landed on the north coast of Africa near Carthage. None of us had any idea we were walking across a sacred battlefield until some bones began moving under our feet...."

Adam Reynolds, 7th grade

Student Journal Presentation

hERODOTUS

"There is another holy bird, called the phoenix, which I have never seen but in pictures. He rarely appears in Egypt— only once in every 500 years.... If the painters describe him truly, his plumage is part golden and part red, and he is very like an eagle in shape and size."

Herodotus

diffusion of knowledge in other forms in recent years. Text as knowledge, or as the representation of knowledge, has been the dominant form of encoding, preserving, and distributing knowledge for centuries in the Western world. Thus if one were to ask a question such as, "What is sophomore biology?" one answer would be to examine the best-selling texts in the field. These texts would help the inquirer to develop a sense of what is typically included and what is typically left out. But how will this change in the coming years? To what extent will the very definition of knowledge and how it is stored and retrieved change?

Knowledge vs. Information

Much of what children are taught in school consists of information. They learn about places, names, events, and dates. They are "taught" alphanumeric "skills" by the dozen. And this is exactly what information is: unconnected bits and pieces that the learner is supposed to make sense of. Some children see or make their own connections, but many do not. Social studies especially, with its bewildering array of facts, is difficult to understand and appreciate. The problem is quite simple: information overload. The solution is even simpler: create meaningful experiences. But

*Maria Patricks,
7th grade*

in spite of how easy it is to identify both problem and solution, few teachers seem to grasp the obvious.

To take an example, for citizenship education to be effective, we must lead our students beyond the horizon of information. One can have information about the three branches of the government and not be a particularly good citizen. One can possess the information that the United States consumes close to forty percent of the world's natural resources and do nothing about it. One can have information about poverty in one's neighborhood and not try to help. Information gathering can resemble spectator sport; watching tennis on television won't make you physically fit or even tired.

Jean Piaget once noted that verbal knowledge is not real knowledge. By that he meant the difference between information and knowledge. Knowledge is based on experience (e.g., hands-on). John Dewey was particularly an advocate of shared experience. He noted that the abstract nature of the curriculum prevented it from being collegial, that is, students and teachers working together in a spirit of cooperation. For a young person to learn to be a good citizen, he or she must work with others, become actively involved, and somehow see him/herself as *contributing* to knowledge as opposed to taking in information. The beneficial outcome

"Do you know what a unicorn is? The word means 'one horn' and this mysterious creature was often mentioned in Greek and Roman myths. People thought it looked like a white horse but with a horn in its forehead. The creature had blue eyes with legs like an antelope and a lion-like tail. It became a symbol of purity. I wish they were real."

Jessica Mills, 6th grade

of such an approach is that the students enjoy learning more, they retain more knowledge, and they get to practice being a participating citizen.

The Journeys approach also allows for the arrangement of knowledge into a natural progression useful for multi-age groupings and to make building-wide themes possible in more meaningful ways. The following example is based on lessons assembled for Unit I (The Golden Age of Greece) from *The Annals of Herodotus, Alexander, and Pliny: Classical World Journeys of Discovery.*

Level:	Intermediate	Middle	Advanced
Travelogue:	Selected primary source accounts from Herodotus of Hallicarnasus		
Sourcebook:			
Language Arts:	Aesop's *Fables*	*The Argonautica*	*The Odyssey*
Social Studies:	"Famous Profiles"	Plutarch I	Plutarch II
Mathematics:	Geometry	Geometry	Geometry
Sciences:	Archimedes & Simple Machines	Erathosthenes & Measurement	Ptolemy & Astronomy
Fine Arts:	Painting (Panaeus)	Architecture (The Acropolis)	Sculpture (Pheidias)
Drama:	Aeschylus, *Agamemnon*	Euripides, *Medeia*	Sophocles, *Oedipus the King*

Such arrangements are possible for any Journey of Discovery unit and engenders student retention of knowledge. Studies of how the brain develops and stores memory indicate that the formulation of natural connections among persons, places, and events forges enduring understandings. For this reason the impact of interdisciplinary units in literature, for example, pointing out the direct associations of Homeric epics with the Herodotus's *Histories*, Shakespeare's play *The Tempest* with the explorations of Sir Francis Drake, and Washington Irving's novels with the Lewis & Clark Expedition, increase student learing over time while engendering a fuller appreciation for our cultural heritage.

II

The Discovery Metaphor

Sidebars:
The Sagas of Leif Ericsson and Early Feudal Kings

LEIF ERICSSON

"The ship was a dragon, built after the one the king had captured in Halogaland. But this ship was far larger, and more carefully put together in all her parts. The king called this ship 'Serpent the Long.' The head and the tail were both gilt.... This ship was the best and most costly ever made in Norway."

Snorri Sturluson, 13th century

At its best an interdisciplinary curriculum represents the quest to put into practice a unified theory of everything educational. An interdisciplinary curriculum is the enterprise par excellence whereby the typically disparate elements of knowledge, teaching, and learning come together to form a coherent whole. This becomes what we can call the fixed idea of interdisciplinary curriculum. The fixed idea here is no different from that which dominates a great symphony. It recurs over and over. In interdisciplinary curriculum, the fixed idea is the discovery of connection. As one discovers connections, the distinction between learners and learning grow indistinct.

The teachers and students whose sights are set on the discovery metaphor are capable of transforming the curriculum from its inert, textbook-dominated condition to one of wonder, investigation, and integrity. Where real discoveries are made, there is always a sense of wonder. And where there is a sense of wonder, there is a sense of anticipation and excitement. These conditions of spiritual renewal are essential if school is to fulfill its promise of a place where students and teachers come together in the name of learning. Integrity is the condition that emerges when education addresses the seamless whole of learning. Integrity is wholeness: wholeness of approach, wholeness of spirit, wholeness of caring-wholeness responding to wholeness, to paraphrase the Chinese philosopher Lao Tzu. This is where the search begins. This is the first step of the journey.

The transformation called for here is enormous. It calls for teachers and students to ask something more of themselves, to transcend the sense of the ordinary, to set out to find something that has not yet been found. To paraphrase Immanuel Kant, the greatest challenge of all is to break the self-imposed shackles of school as a place where the barriers to excellence are pre-existent.

The interdisciplinary curriculum integrates. It integrates people, ideas, and learning. This is why the metaphor of curriculum as a journey of discovery is so compelling. The great journeys of discovery that leap from the pages of history inspiring countless generations are nearly always shared ventures into the unknown. Curriculum as a known artifact, already known to teachers, to be learned (and therefore known at least for a time) by students, diminishes the noble character of teaching and learning. It does so for two reasons. The first reason is that curriculum as known artifact robs learning of its discovery potential. And secondly, it divides teachers from students when they should be together in the shared quest. Curriculum as a shared venture into the unknown, fraught with all the perils of an expedition, whose goals are clear but whose achievement and results can only be determined and understood upon reflection, creates a qualitatively different sense of what it means to teach and learn. This is what Dewey meant when he wrote that, finally, the learner and the curriculum are actually two ends of the same continuum.

The Discovery Metaphor

It is instructive for us to probe the discovery metaphor in teaching and learning. In the annals of discovery, there are two senses of the word. The first sense of discovery is that of "Big D" Discovery. The second is that of "little d" discovery. Big D discoveries are world-class, original discoveries, the kind that make their way into the history books and the biographies and whichtake on epic proportions. Little d discoveries are the kind that you and I make along the way with little or no claim to originality but which are immensely satisfying. The fact that someone else may have previously made the same or a similar discovery does not take away from the pleasure we feel when we have found out something for ourselves. This is the beginning of self-discovery.

In the curriculum experience at its best, there is a happy convergence of Big D and little d discoveries. A curriculum that is

"Leif said, 'Why are you so late in coming home, foster-father? Tyrk said, 'I did not go much farther than you, but I found something new to report. I found grapevines and grapes!' ...[A]nd when spring came they made ready and sailed away with a favorable wind. Leif named the land after its special product and called it Vineland."

Flateyjarbok,
9th century

focused on the discoveries of Isaac Newton, Lewis and Clark, Leonardo da Vinci, or Marie Curie, for example, leaves plenty of room for students and teachers to make their own discoveries. The spirit is the same. The quest is not qualitatively different. Again, the theme of integration emerges. Text is merged with experience. Students and teachers become members of the expedition: they are there with Marco Polo on the Old Silk Road, with Captain Cook at Botany Bay, with Madam Curie in her laboratory.

But there is more to the discovery metaphor than vicarious experience, valuable as that may be in enriching our lives. There is the sense of discovery that occurs when a gifted teacher insists against the odds that the students should become artists, poets, scientists, geographers, and mathematicians. And the quest begins. There is the discovery that happens when a child sits down on the floor with a map spread out before her and her fingers begin ever so slowly to traverse the ancient caravan routes across Central Asia, and she realizes for the first time in her life that a map is a tool of wonder and imagination. There is the discovery that emerges when a child collects botanic specimens and preserves and classifies them in just the same way that explorers before him did. And there is the discovery that takes place when a

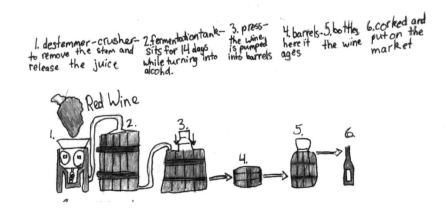

young learner is filled with emotion after learning the sad story of Chief Joseph's retreat.

The Power of Shared Experience

Best of all there are the discoveries that occur along the way in shared experience. Students discover that working together on projects too big for one person opens up undreamed possibilities. This is the stuff of pageants, fairs, and field trips. One of the abiding tragedies of our time is the growing privatism of human experience. The willingness to sequester ourselves alone at home in front of a television, computer, or video screen draws us into a vortex of increasing isolation from the give and take of shared existence.

Students and teachers who work together on shared adventures of discovery experience something that doesn't happen when they work alone. It is the transcendent moment that cannot be achieved in isolation. It is the feeling of camaraderie and esprit de corps that happens to members of clubs, athletic teams, scout groups, church groups, and other social groups. Group experience that achieves true integration meets a deeper human need for affiliation, belonging, and friendship. So deep is this learning that it defies explanation. Only experience defines it.

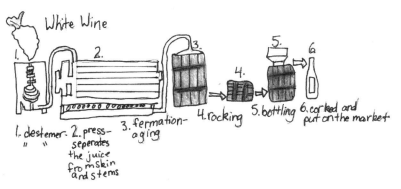

The Winemaking Process
by Gavin McKee,
6th grade

Journeys
Journal
Entry

"Life in ancient times across North America was a constant struggle. It involved following the herds and hunting other game with techniques that required great skill and knowledge of animal life. This time when humans first arrived to about 9000 B.C. has come to be known as the period of Clovis Culture."

Aaron Howell,
7th grade

LEIF ERICSSON

"Now when the king was warring, the men found a goodman with a great herd-dog. The hound ran all about the herd in a way all thought wonderfully wise. Then the king asked the goodman if he would sell his hound and gave him a gold ring. That dog was named Vigi, and was the best of dogs. Olaf had him for a long time."

Snorri Sturluson

What is the Curriculum?

An interdisciplinary curriculum is an integrated curriculum, and to understand the implications of such an idea, we ourselves must do some exploration of the curriculum and its potential to serve teachers and students. First of all there is the idea of curriculum as a disciplinary construct. By this it is meant that the scholarly disciplines serve as the basis of the course of study. There is nothing particularly new or insightful about this observation. It is merely a way of acknowledging that such disciplines as the natural sciences, English, mathematics, history, art, etc., are the building blocks of what is to be learned at school. This is different from saying that they are ends in themselves, but that subtle point is too often lost.

If one accepts as reasonable the assumption that the scholarly disciplines are a place to start, and they are, then the question of how to configure them into something meaningful for teachers and students arises. The time-honored approach comes from the universities. There, at levels of advanced scholarship, disciplines are treated as separated entities for purposes of thorough examination and development by professors and students. The practice is sometimes of questionable value even at this level, but it has, by and large, served a rather useful purpose of producing scholars and advancing the frontiers of knowledge.

In 1892, when the then fledgling National Education Association (NEA) commissioned the Committee of Ten, chaired by Harvard University President Charles Eliot, to produce a coherent secondary school curriculum, the Committee took its cues from the university curriculum of the time. This, of course, was a curriculum composed of separate subjects taught to students by expert teachers in roughly 50-minute time periods. The teachers' expertise was found in their knowledge of subject matter and not so much in their teaching ability. In essence, the Committee took the university curriculum and presented it to the secondary school. Whether or not this was wise has been debated for more then a century. But the Committee's influence was powerful, and we still basically follow its recommendations today.

The disciplinary approach to curriculum in schools rests on several interesting assumptions, not all of which may be valid. The idea is to assign teachers who are more or less experts in a single subject to instruct students daily in a given discipline. Students are expected to attend to that discipline for an appointed time, generally about an hour, before they move on to their next class which repeats the pattern with different material. This happens about five times per day. The whole notion is that students, guided by a knowledgeable teacher, can concentrate their attention on, say, earth science, in some degree of depth thereby themselves becoming, if not experts, at least reasonably well acquainted with the subject at hand.

Over time a student who takes enough of these courses and who learns from them is said to have a general education, more in fact devoted to breadth of coverage than to depth. Of course, there are some subjects in the curriculum that are not disciplinary, for example, home economics or word processing. They are considered to be practical arts or life skills courses and are considered to be quite valuable, but the core of the curriculum is comprised of the various separately taught and separately learned disciplines. The reason the student is said to have a general education is two-fold: on the one hand, he or she has taken a wide range of classes, and on the other hand he or she is expected to be able to link the learning from the various classes into a coherent whole, or to be able to achieve what might be called a sense of integrity of his or her learning. This is a noble assumption—one that is basic to the foundation of a democratic society which can work well only with an educated citizenry.

We know that it is common to teach subjects separately, and we know the rationale: a knowledgeable teacher offering an in-depth focus for students. What we are less sure of is how successful this approach is for senior high school students, much less for middle school or elementary students. The question must be asked whether the curriculum is best delivered this way or perhaps in some alternate form. In truth, conclusive proof of the superiority of one means of curriculum structure over another is lacking for a

"Hi, my name is Kathy here at KWWY radio and I am going to tell you about my favorite dog breed, the Siberian husky. These dogs are compact and powerful with terrific stamina. They were introduced to the rest of the world by the Siberian Chukchi tribe as an all-purpose sled dog. Using these animals for sledding was not for fun originally because they were used to get medicine for children in Alaska sick with diptheria."

Casey Miller,
6th grade

Alfred the Great

variety of reasons, and as often as not we are left with competing points of view rather than final arguments.

The single disciplinary approach can be likened to a daily reading of the comics in a newspaper. Each comic strip or cartoon is self-contained, having nothing to do with the others. The reader merely superficially considers one before moving on to the next one. Except for a pompous few devoted to political satire, there is no pretense of serious teaching by the writer/illustrator or of serious learning by the reader whose only goal is to be temporarily amused. No connections are even expected to occur between or among the various comics, and no common themes appear except as they might coincidentally touch on topics of interest in the society at large. For the comics, this is fine, but what about the school curriculum?

Toward a Changed Structure

For starters, the school curriculum is serious business, and the purpose of the comics is entertainment. Beyond that, however, several arguments for changing the structure and nature of the curriculum for school students can be advanced. The first of these arguments has to do with the strange historical phenomenon that has resulted in the combination of a university-type subject mat-

3-Dimensional Palace Facade, posterboard cutouts

ter delivery system, right down to the fifty-minute periods with a program of custody or daycare. Let us take a moment to examine this issue.

The reason that university courses are fifty minutes to one hour in length is that this is about how long it takes to deliver a well conceived lecture followed by a few questions from the audience. The idea is that students might attend from one to three lectures on any given day, generally with time between classes. It is not unusual for students to find that on some days they do not even have classes. And when they do, the number of hours is limited. What the students do between classes is up to them. They might study or do some research in the library; they might play tennis; they might meet friends for coffee. Regardless of what they do, there is time built in for them to distance themselves from and reflect on what they have learned in class or to recover from the concentration of listening, taking notes, or discussing issues. The university curriculum is simply not configured in such a way as to force students to take one class after another each day for six hours. To expect such a thing would be to ignore the most fundamental principles of learning. It would create a frenetic pace rather than the more leisurely pace required of serious learning. Bear in mind that the Greek word *schola*, meant, in ancient times, a place of leisure, set aside from the world. The Greeks, acting on this

Feudal Britain,
Samantha Bammes,
6th grade

"In each tree [of understanding] I saw something I needed at home. Therefore, I exhort all who are able, to direct their steps to the self-same forest where I cut .... Let them there obtain for themselves, and load their wagons with fir branches, so they may weave a strong wall, and build a rare house, and dwell therein in joy and comfort...."
Alfred the Great

metaphor, produced Socrates, Plato, and Aristotle. But they didn't spend their whole day going from one disconnected class to another.

The curious thing about all of this is that university students are more mature learners than school students, and they represent a more select, academically talented clientele than one finds in the typical public school. Why, therefore, do we ask less of university students than of children and adolescents in terms of number of class hours per week? And why do we give university students more time to reflect on their learning than we give to younger people who reason would dictate require *more* time to reflect on what they have been taught?

Of course, the reason why we have traditionally kept younger students busy moving from one class to the next has nothing to do with learning or with time for reflective thought. It is a daycare or custodial arrangement. Thus the fifty-minute period is primarily an artifact of university level instruction placed into a situation where there is little or nothing in the way of rationale to support it other than tradition. Granted, our students need some form of responsible daycare. We simply cannot turn them loose like university students between classes. But think about the mind-numbing process of sending ordinary achievers from class to class, hour after hour in a way that higher achieving university students are not asked to do. At some point, the benefits of instruction are overwhelmed by overload in such a way that no serious person would acknowledge as being intellectually stimulating.

Thus we have a situation where younger, unselected students are asked to take more classes per day in the name of learning than mature, academically selected students do. That is, they are expected to absorb more lectures and presentations than their older, more selected counterparts. Those who doubt that students are spending their class time listening to lectures should check the *research data* which show the single most probable classroom event at the secondary school level is teacher talk, and at the elementary level, seatwork. And as though that were not enough, we allow no open time between classes where students might reflect, study, rest, or gather socially.

And lastly, we offer students separate courses expecting them to do what their teachers do not apparently do; that is, tie the knowledge, skills, and values of the various courses together into some kind of coherent whole. Theoretically, at least, the idea of general education is that the various components assume a measure of wholeness. Perhaps a few students see the relationships among and between separate subjects, but most surely do not. If this were really an important goal, one might well reason, then teachers ought to plan together and to offer courses that have obvious links with one another. This could be accomplished through synchronized assignments, cross-disciplinary projects, and other similar means.

Integrated Curriculum as an Answer

The obvious answer to the deep-seated problem of a "fractionalized" curriculum, one which seemingly starts nowhere and goes nowhere, remaining disconnected from life, is the integrated approach to teaching and learning. There is nothing new about integration. It has been around in one form or another for a long time. Unfortunately, it has not always delivered on its promise. Let's examine why this might be and what can be done to remedy the situation.

We begin with a modest assumption: separately taught disciplines can be connected in such a way that they can offer strategic support to one another while maintaining their own integrity and sense of proportion. This is a modest assumption but one that is often ignored or violated in the rush to combine subjects. To address this assumption we must pose a fundamental question. How can the various subjects that traditionally contribute individually to the curriculum instead contribute collectively?

The Journeys of Discovery interdisciplinary curriculum for students in grades four through eight is based on themes that have a rich potential for depth of content and which demand the best of each contributory discipline. The discovery theme has sustaining

"Pearls of Wisdom"
Never say the word "hate" when talking about people.
Be polite among strangers.
Always help elderly people.
Never say "never."

Sterling Hampton, 6th grade

ALFRED the GREAT

"I do not know whether I, after the parting of the body and the soul, shall ever know more than now of all that which I have long wished to know. I cannot find anything better than to know, and anything worse than to be ignorant."

Alfred the Great

curricular value, and its variations are virtually unlimited. Thus major texts and subtexts emerge. While the theme is played out principally around the recorded journeys of such luminaries as Herodotus of the Ancient World, Marco Polo of the Medieval World, James Cook of the World of the Enlightenment, and Lewis and Clark of the New World, a number of related journeys complement the major curricular themes.

The idea that curriculum could be organized around the theme of discovery and discoverers is meant to be exemplary of the content/conceptual potential of interdisciplinary approaches in general as much as anything else. Other potentially engaging themes could as well include invention and inventors, adventures and adventurers, creativity and creators, leadership and leaders, etc. Most importantly we must choose something that can draw upon all curricular areas with authenticity and which has the capability to join the separate disciplines as contributors to large projects and thoughtful activities.

One of the goals of any good interdisciplinary curriculum is to bring students and teachers closer to the frontiers of knowledge through access to original source materials, principally in the form of diaries, journals, logs, and other forms of first person accounts. Taken on these terms, the curriculum has the potential to turn students into historians, writers, geographers, dramatists, math-

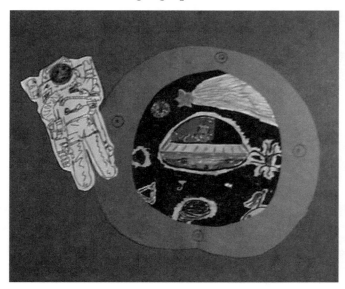

Young Astronaut Poster

ematicians, scientists, musicians, and artists. Far too often students and teachers work with processed textbook accounts of the great reach of the human spirit, denying themselves the pleasure and excitement of taking source material and trying to make sense of it for themselves. This is where the encounter with the true spirit of education begins, with one's thoughts about something worthwhile.

But this is only the beginning. The teacher's task is to figure out the potential for such original source material to connect with the skills and knowledge-students will need in an uncertain future. This is the role of problem solving, the mysterious business of preparation, incubation, illumination, and verification. But teachers have to make sure that something else happens beyond the choice of worthwhile content studied in a problem-solving mode. They must ensure that integration occurs not merely with curriculum content, but with the people who study the curriculum as well.

The first line of integration must occur within the teaching staff. It is not acceptable for teachers to withdraw into their respective shells of subject matter expertise while making the disclaimer that they don't know much if anything about other areas of the curriculum. In the interdisciplinary approach, each teacher must see him/herself as an integral part of a strategic whole. Each teacher

Journeys Journal Entry

"What I would really like to know is whether or not there is life on Mars. The air and temperature there would not allow us to survive but I would like to take one breath and see what it is like. It may be possible for people to travel there soon so...."

John Bonnington, 7th grade

Planet	Diameter	SGS	aa	miles from Sun	miles from town
Mercury	3,000	8	.4	36,000	15
Venus	7,500	2.1	.7	67,000	.3
Eearth	7,900	2.2	1	93,000	.4
Mars	4,200	1.2	1.5	141,000	.6
Jupiter	90,000	24.9	5	484,000	2
Saturn	75,000	20.1	10	880,000	4
Uranis	32,000	8.3	20	1,786,000	8
Neptune	30,000	8.3	30	2,799,000	12
Pluto	1,400	.4	40	3,666,000	16
Sun (star) alfa Centari	865,000	237.6	0	0 4.3 Lightyears	0

Calculations to place planet models with relative size and shape within 16 miles of school,
David Corder,
6th grade

chARLEmAGHE

"Charlemagne practiced his faith with great devotion and piety, for he had been brought up this way since earliest childhood. This explains why he built a cathedral of such beauty at Aachen, decorating it with gold and silver, with lamps, and with lattices and doors of solid bronze. Its marble columns were brought from Rome and Ravenna."

*Einard,
9th century*

must bring a special expertise or interest to the table, but each teacher must also engage the other areas of the curriculum thoughtfully. This begins to happen when teachers talk and plan with each other about an important crosscutting theme, one that truly demands the insights of each teacher and his/her specialty. Thus teachers must experience integration if they want to integrate the subject they teach. An important rule of thumb to keep in mind about integration is "first people, then subjects."

Once the teaching staff begins to feel integrated, and they have chosen a worthwhile theme that calls on the various disciplines, the next step is to commit to integrating students. At its best, interdisciplinary teaching and learning is project oriented. The best projects, like the best journeys of discovery, take teamwork. Somehow the feeling that we need each other in order to carry out the visionary projects that will be undertaken throughout the year needs to be communicated to students. Interdisciplinary curriculum must call on all the disciplines in order to be successful, and more importantly, it must call upon all students to share with each other their gifts, talents, energy, good will, and hard work.

Now, having integrated subject matter, faculty, and students, what else is left? This is no time to stop. Here the parents and other interested community members must be integrated into the curriculum. It can be done, and it must be done in order to achieve the highest levels of success. One of the surest ways to raise achievement in a school is to involve interested adults in meaningful ways. Where parents feel informed and involved, a host of problems are diminished. The school that can bring families together around the abiding ideas of a thoughtful curriculum is a school that not only will prosper academically but also will find support in other areas when it needs it.

III

The Discovery Experience

Sidebars:
Eleanor of Aquitaine and the Crusade of the Kings

ELEANOR R.

Interdisciplinary approaches to the curriculum are improved when they are supported by discovery learning. Discovery learning places the center of gravity with the student rather than with the teacher or the material to be learned. Thus the curriculum has the potential to become a course of study (which was its original intent) instead of a course of instruction or a body of content to be learned for its own sake.

The Role of Leadership

In the discovery experience, students must take the initiative for their learning. The teacher's role shifts from teller and director to organizer and guide. For the purposes of the Journeys of Discovery curriculum this change in metaphor is significant. The teacher assumes much the same role that Lewis and Clark assumed in their epic journey, or that any other good leaders assume. Their role, and likewise that of a discovery-oriented teacher, is to ensure that the trip is well-organized, that preparation, support, and follow-through are in place as much as possible as students and teachers together venture across an uncharted landscape of learning. It is also incumbent upon a teacher in this context to show the way just as a good guide leads the way. The metaphor of teacher as guide allows for leadership under a lead explorer whose experience, know-how, and insight model and facilitate the processes of inquiry, invention, documentation, and creativity.

Good leadership is a balancing act that provides structure without being overbearing, that points the way while recognizing that more than one path may get someone from here to there. These are fundamental changes in teacher role, and they are not easy changes for some teachers to make. One way to think of the teacher's role is as that of the leader of an expedition. The changes are often difficult for students to make as well, particularly those students whose success has been based in large measure on their skill at doing what they are told to do. The problem ultimately for "other-directed" students is that it is difficult for them to learn on their own. They may be good at responding to direction and to completing assignments given to them by teachers, but this represents an impoverished sense of what it means to learn. Discoverers, on the other hand, need not wait around to be told what to do. They know how to move ahead by posing questions, constructing hypotheses, gathering data, trying to make sense of it, and by reaching conclusions. So the fundamental, underlying goal structure changes from other-directed to self-directed. For both teachers and students, the goal becomes enabling: to set oneself free to become a self-sustaining learner whose desire to learn carries on beyond the school experience into lifelong learning.

Graham Wallas on Problem-Solving and Discovery

Many scholars have attempted to capture the essence of the discovery experience, but probably no one has equaled the insight of Graham Wallas when it comes to reducing what happens to a few well-chosen words. Wallas conceived of the discovery process as something that happens in four identifiable stages. The stages are not necessarily linear in function, and there is no doubt a considerable amount of slipping back and forth from stage to stage as one discovers something. He called the stages *preparation*, *incubation*, *illumination*, and *verification*. The words are so descriptive as to nearly speak for themselves. Still, let's spend a little time with each.

Preparation

The first stage in the discovery process is preparation. This stage is so often underestimated and overlooked by the less-than-seri-

Journeys Journal Entry

"Human language sets us apart from all other living things. Without language it would be difficult to survive because without one's particular form of communication there would be little understanding of special knowledge that is handed down from generation to generation."

*Annie Kjack,
7th grade*

RICHARD III

ous that most attempts at discovery learning lead to frustration and abandonment, resulting in the "we tried that ..." syndrome so familiar to teachers. Preparation represents a kind of blend of attitude and information. The old adage that chance favors the prepared mind is useful to remember in this context. An attitude of openness, especially to the seemingly outlandish and impossible is necessary, but it must be supported by a desire to know one's object of study.

The somewhat apocryphal story of Isaac Newton's discovery of the so-called law of gravity while sitting under an apple tree is a good example of attitude and information coming together. When the apple fell to earth from the tree, Newton employed his deep knowledge of the attraction of one mass to another, the greater mass pulling the lesser mass toward its center. But people had long been aware of this. The key was Newton's openness to the cause as well as the easily observable result. Thus it was that Newton realized before others that the attraction of one object to another actually represents a universal principle that works in any setting anywhere. Other scientists, including Galileo and Kepler, had done earlier work. Thus Newton's knowledge was more than just his own scholarly judgment and intuition. He was able to take the existent knowledge and refine it into a mathematical formula that illustrates every particle of matter in the universe attracts every

Horned Owl
Jared Wolfe,
7th grade

other particle with a force directly proportional to the product of their masses and inversely proportional to the square of the distance between them. He expressed the formula mathematically as:

$$F = \frac{G\,(m_1 m_2)}{D^2}$$

where F is the force of attraction, m and m are the masses of the two objects, D is the distance between the two objects, and G is a universal gravitational constant. The point to underscore is that Newton depended heavily upon knowledge he had gained from a variety of sources as a way of preparing for this discovery, and he still would not have made it had he not been open to the possibilities. Knowledge is essential to discovery, but not inert knowledge learned merely as an exercise or to pass an exam; knowledge that is organic is the kind of knowledge that sustains the learner with a spirit of openness to new ideas. We'll return to this example later as we examine subsequent stages of the Graham Wallas discovery model.

The discovery metaphor is brought to concrete example in the epic trek of Lewis and Clark. Theirs was to be a discovery process that unfolded over several years during which time they ranged out to the Pacific and back. These were resourceful people to be sure, but the *preparations* they took for the journey were in large

"There once was a castle with a beautiful garden. This garden was very special because it held the king's tree of golden apples. All was well in the kingdom until one day a guard noticed that apples had been taken from the tree. The king's son came to investigate and was surprised to see near the tree a large yet delicate golden feather that glowed...."

Jessica Appleton, 6th grade

Robin in Flight
Karl Scheuerman, 7th grade

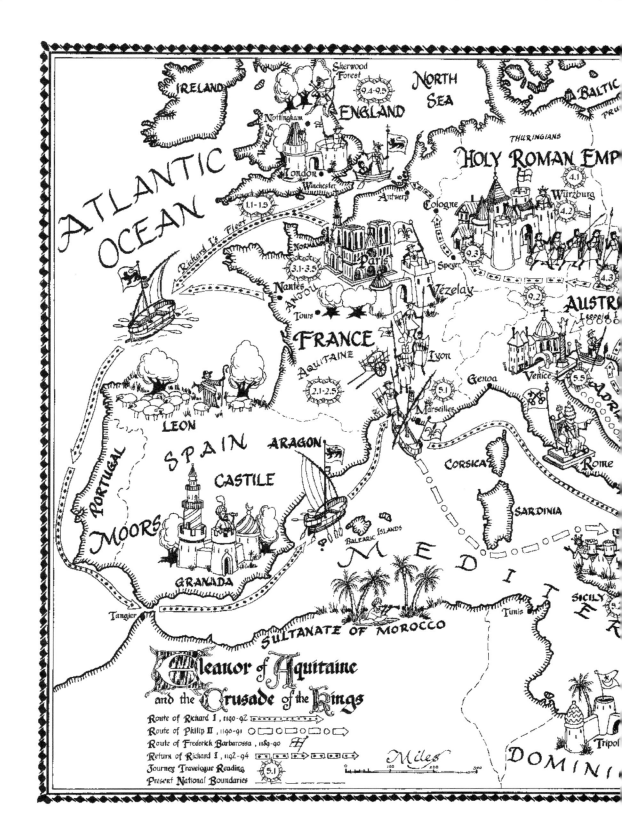

IRELAND

NORTH SEA

Sherwood Forest
9.4-9.5

ENGLAND

Nottingham

Wales

London

Winchester

1.1-1.5

Antwerp

Cologne

THURINGIANS

HOLY ROMAN EMP

4.1

Würzburg

4.2

9.3

Speyer

4.3

ATLANTIC OCEAN

Richard I's Fleet

NORMA
3.1-3.5

Nantes
ANJOU
Tours

Paris

Vezelay

9.2

AUSTR
Leopold I

FRANCE

AQUITAINE

2.1-2.5

Lyon

Genoa

Venice

5.5

5.1

Marseilles

Rome

PORTUGAL

SPAIN

ARAGON

CASTILE

LEON

CORSICA

SARDINIA

MOORS

GRANADA

Balearic Islands

MEDITER

Tangier

SULTANATE OF MOROCCO

Tunis

SICILY

Eleanor of Aquitaine
and the Crusade of the Kings

Route of Richard I , 1190-92
Route of Philip II , 1190-91
Route of Frederick Barbarossa , 1189-90
Return of Richard I , 1192-94
Journey Travelogue Reading   5.1
Present National Boundaries

Miles
100   200   500

DOMINI

Tripoli

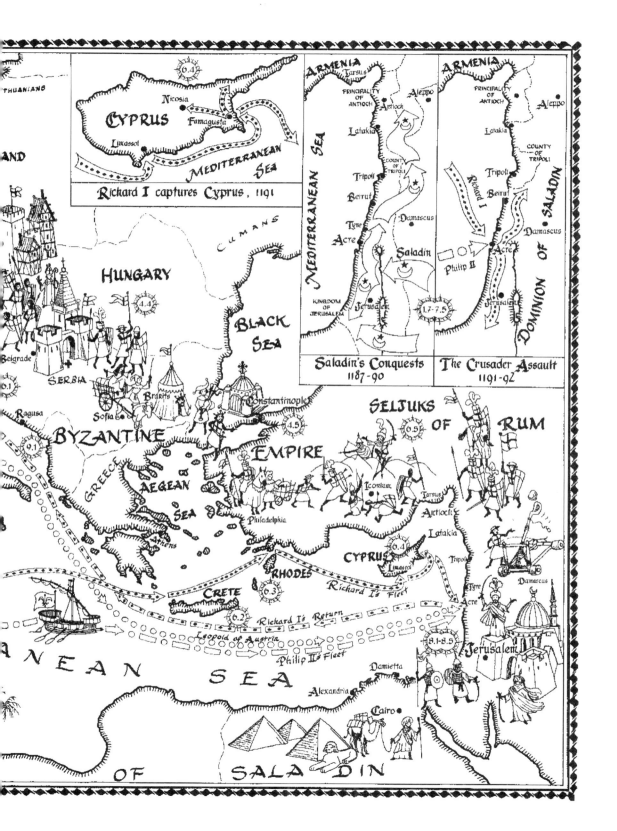

Richard I captures Cyprus, 1191

Saladin's Conquests 1187-90

The Crusader Assault 1191-92

F. BARBAROSSA

"The season of the year was now ripening towards autumn and the constellation Libra was balancing the day and night in nearly equal lengths. The magnificent emperor [Frederick Barbarossa] marched to take up his winter quarters at Adrianople...."

Geoffrey of Vinsauf, 1189

measure a key to its ultimate success. The same could be said for the journeys of Marco Polo and James Cook.

This is not the place to furnish all the details of preparation that went into Lewis and Clark's journey of discovery, but this brief and typical passage of instruction from President Thomas Jefferson to Captain Meriwether Lewis illustrates how seriously this stage of discovery was taken: "Your observations are to be taken with great pains & accuracy, to be entered distinctly & intelligibly for others as well as yourself, to comprehend all the elements necessary, with the aid of the usual tables, to fix the latitude and longitude of the places at which they were taken & are to be rendered to the war office, for the purpose of having the calculations made concurrently by the proper persons with the U.S...."

The fact is Lewis and Clark ventured over some areas where others had already been, but the difference between their true journey of discovery and the wanderings of others illustrates the power of preparation. A final point about preparation in the discovery process is in order. Discovery by its very nature takes one into the unknown, and the unknown is always fraught with peril. Whether we consider young learners attempting to discover on their own without being told all the answers or whether we consider the triumphs and disasters that have befallen both the American and

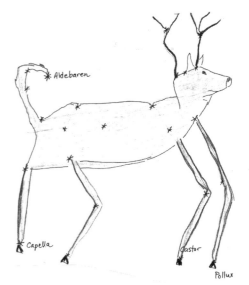

Mikaya the Deer,
Marianne Adams,
6th grade

Russian space programs, even careful preparation is no guarantee of a secure voyage. But the very lack of a guarantee is the key to the excitement of the discovery approach to learning.

Incubation

The mysterious process known as incubation represents Wallas' second stage of discovery. This stage has been the undoing of more than one would-be discoverer, whether teacher or student. Good preparation has a sense of activity about it as one organizes the adventure. Incubation, on the other hand, is a kind of waiting game, as the image of a hen sitting on a nest of eggs would suggest. Actually though, much is happening during this seemingly passive stage. This is a time to ponder and consider a problem, to allow oneself the luxury of thinking ahead in time while reflecting back on what has happened so far. In some respects this is an unpredictable, nonlinear process that can give the appearance of time wasted.

Incubation is necessary because it slows one down from the temptation to move ahead too quickly following the preparation stage. This is a time to be deliberate, patient, and thoughtful. It can also be a time of reflection and even second-guessing of one's original premise. To attempt to rush this stage is to force the pro-

*Designing
Star Charts*

*Journeys
Journal
Entry*

"I think astronomy is interesting and I would like to learn more about how to become an aerospace technician for NASA. These people work on a team to create spacecraft. To do this you have to be good at math and science and know how to operate electrical and mechanical equipment. You also have to know how to get along with other people...."

*Manuel Ruiz,
8th grade*

"In these maritime parts there were also numbers of beasts of the forest. They leaped up between our feet from the long grass and thick copses and many were caught, not by design, but came in their way by chance. As each night came round, a sort of creature attacked us, commonly called tarrentes, which creeps on the ground and has most venomous stings."

Geoffrey of Vinsauf, 1192

cess. It makes no more sense than to try to speed up the blossoming of a flower or the hatching of an egg. In concrete form, a teacher and class who have been writing journals of their own discoveries as they study the explorations of Lewis and Clark need to spend time reflecting on the meaning of what they are doing.

In some sense, the idea of incubation is akin to metacognition, or thinking about the activities, processes, etc., in which one becomes so busily engaged. It is useful to remember that one definition of a fanatic is a person who redoubles his efforts having lost sight of the original goal. It is not unusual to see teachers who are thoroughly committed to working harder without reflecting on what it means to work well. Perhaps the so-called "add-on" curriculum from which we all suffer is a product of our failure to reflectively consider what it is we are trying to accomplish.

A few years ago a book was published, one that sold in the multiple thousands, titled *Teach More, Faster*. The thesis of this book for teachers was that they could cover more information and skills if only they were more efficient. The book showed them how to become more efficient. Perhaps some application of the incubation process would have led teachers to consider whether teaching and learning are really about efficiency. "Teach less, more slowly, teach it well," is more to the point.

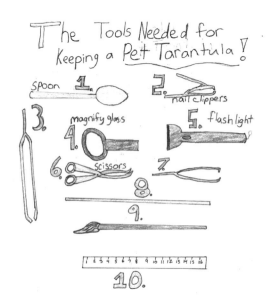

Illumination

The stage called "illumination" by Wallas is perhaps the best known aspect of discovery. This is where the proverbial light bulb comes on, the kind cartoonists like to show lighting up above the thinker's head. This is where the discovery takes place. It is the time of insight, of new knowledge, of things known which were unknown. What was unclear or shrouded in mystery is now perceived or has at least become less mysterious.

Maybe the best known case of illumination in recorded history is the legendary story of Archimedes, who ran naked through the streets of Athens shouting "Eureka" when he realized that an object will displace its density when placed in water. Apparently, Archimedes had been "incubating" in the bathtub trying to solve a problem of determining whether a crown made for the king was in fact solid gold. The answer came to him in a flash when he realized that all objects displace their density in water, and gold had a certain density.

Thomas Edison used to practice the incubation stage during those brief catnaps he would take at his laboratory in Menlo Park, New Jersey. Edison, who typically slept only a few hours at night, would sometimes sit down in an easy chair for a short rest. He would hold a steel ball bearing in each hand, and as he relaxed

1. **Spoons are needed to coax out spiders, change soil, or remove leftovers.**

2. **Nail clippers are used for clipping.**

3. **Tongs are used to place food in the case.**

4. **A magnifying glass shows the spider's remarkable details.**

5. **A flashlight can help you find an escaped spider at night!**

Journeys Journal Entry

"My cousin has a pet tarantula and keeps it in a terrarium in her bedroom. I can't imagine being able to go to sleep just knowing that creature is so close! She says they are harmless but that is not the case with other spiders who live around here. Two that you would not want to have for a pet are the black widow and brown recluse."

Jay Neiman,
7th grade

SALADIN

"Beware of bloodshed; do not trust in that, for spilled blood never sleeps. Strive to gain the hearts of thy subjects and watch over all of their interests, for you are appointed to look after their welfare. Others have called me great because I have won their hearts by gentleness and kindness."

Sultan Saladin, 1193

and dozed off the ball bearings would drop onto tin pie pans placed strategically on the floor below. The sound would wake him, and he would immediately write down his thoughts. Recent brain-function research supports Edison's method, because the brain secretes higher levels of theta waves, associated with creativity, as we fall asleep than during normal waking hours.

The problem-solving cycle is completed when we are able to document, "prove," or otherwise verify our results. The problem-solver reaches the moment of discovery in the illumination stage, but still must figure out ways to confirm that the findings are indeed sound. Sometimes this involves replicating the study or searching for further evidence. Often the verification stage is reached when we can show that verification was not reached by chance. In other words, our findings should hold up under repeated scrutiny. Tables, charts, graphs, maps, and written summaries of findings are typically used to illustrate our results from which appropriate conclusions can be drawn. The conclusions are usually presented in the form of inferences or even generalizations.

"Verification" is actually a tentative matter in true problem-solving. Our search is for the truth, but the "truth" in such matters is tentative and limited to answering the specific questions we posed. An exception sometimes occurs when serendipitous encounters yield unexpected findings for which we had not even posed questions. But more often than not, verification leads to new questions and further inquiry. In this sense, problem-solving processes tend to function more in spiral than linear fashion. Questions lead to answers which in turn lead to questions. This process is the beauty of the enterprise and central to expansive learning.

IV

Inquiry and Understanding

Sidebars:
The Travels of Marco Polo and Ibn Battuta

MARCO POLO

"The Great Khan gave Misters Nicolo and Maffeo Polo a tablet of gold on which was inscribed that the ambassadors should be supplied with everything needful in all the countries through which they should pass. On their arrival [in Venice] Mister Nicolo found that his wife was dead and that she had left behind her a son fifteen years of age whose name was Marco."

*Marco Polo,
13th century*

A comment often made by schoolteachers goes something like this: "I'd love to do inquiry teaching, but I'm not sure that I even know what it is." Also, we hear comments such as: "I guess I've been doing inquiry for years; we just never called it that."

Part of the problem is the absence of a publicly agreed upon definition of "inquiry." Of course, inquiry is done in science, the humanities, mathematics, and other subjects as well as social science, and in each case the emphasis is somewhat different. Let us pose a definition that should be a useful place to start. *Inquiry is a process in which we pose questions about some phenomenon and attempt to discover meaning by making inferences about the answers that we obtain.* So, to do inquiry one typically begins by posing an empirical question, that is, one that can be answered through the gathering and evaluating of data. An example of this might be, "What was childhood like for our grandparents?" or, "What simple machines are used at home?" Once we have our question (in this case a historical question) we can begin to think about gathering the information (data) necessary to give us answers. The techniques of data gathering, whether a survey, a reading of old diaries, interviews with grandparents, or an investigation of secondary sources could all be considered forms of inquiry.

The questions we pose are what guide our inquiry. The answers we obtain are what inform our discovery. This is the relationship between inquiry and discovery. One inquires in order to discover. Inquiry questions are questions that can be answered by gathering information and putting the information together in new ways.

This may sound rather simple, but take a moment to contrast inquiry questions with philosophical questions. A philosophical question cannot be answered primarily by gathering information. If we were to ask, "What is the most beautiful color?" we may find opinions ranging from blue, red, green, etc., but no amount of information will yield a definitive answer to the question, which is one of personal preference. A related question based on inquiry procedures might be, "What is the most popular 'school colors' choice of students in our school?" A survey of color preferences or an interview session with focus groups would allow us to discover the range of opinion or choice on the matter.

More often inquiry and discovery are contrasted with the kind of traditional learning that goes on at school. This type of learning, based on what is called didactic teaching, involves teaching students specific knowledge, a skill, for example a particular mathematics operation and then having them follow up by practicing the operation in the form of problems or exercises. Didactic teaching in history might typically involve having students read a passage from a textbook or listen to a lecture followed either by a discussion or some form of written assignment. There is, of course, nothing wrong with didactic teaching when it is done in moderation. In fact it is a useful way to teach certain skills and knowledge. The biggest learning problem associated with didactic teaching is its overuse. When it becomes a day-in, day-out routine, it loses its potential to reach students in meaningful ways. This is often the beginning of such commonly held student attitudes as, "Social studies was always boring for me because it was just a bunch of names, dates, and places." Or, "I never could see the point of all the math problems we had to work on." These, of course, are perceptions of reality. The same experience might have affected someone else differently, but the truth is that in far too many cases the perception of school life as boring, irrelevant, etc. is closely associated with an overabundance of didacticism.

So, inquiry and discovery involve question posing, data gathering, analysis, and, always, a search for meaning. We ask a question. We gather information. And we try to make sense of our information. We can ask questions about the past (historical inquiry). We can ask questions about the present (descriptive in-

Journeys Journal Entry

"Not very long ago we found in the attic a large wooden chest with tin-covered sides full of papers. We opened it up and rummaged through the stuff that still smelled of moth balls. Among the papers were two antique cards that had a moving part held by a brass brad. Written on them in beautiful ink script was...."

Jared Bailey, 6th grade

MARCO POLO

"Russia is a very great province, lying towards the north. The people are Christians and follow the Greek doctrine. There are several kings in the country and they have a language of their own. Both men and women are very handsome... with long, fair hair. They have many fine and valuable furs, such as sable, ermine, vair, ercolin, and fox, the largest and finest in the world and also much wax."

Marco Polo, 1272

quiry). Or we can establish special conditions in order to study something (experimental inquiry).

Inquiry and discovery invariably involve problem solving. These terms are closely linked. If we decided to answer the question, "What is a typical school day for Japanese students?" we would try to describe life in a Japanese school. Therefore, this would be *descriptive* research. If we asked the question, "What was a typical school day for children in Colonial New England?" we have posed an *historical* question. If we asked the question, "How will our classroom be different if we change the seating arrangement into a circle?" then we have posed an *experimental* question. If we asked the question, "What extracurricular programs would the students in our school like the most?" we have posed a *survey* question. Notice that all these questions can be "answered" by gathering information and discovering meaning in the information. Thus an inquiring question, once posed, sets the stage for problem solving.

Inquiry and discovery as teaching/learning modes are fundamental to the Journeys of Discovery curriculum. The program simply will not work without them. This is why students in Journeys of Discovery must have access to original source material including such rich sources of information as artists' sketches, musicians' scores, mathematicians' proofs, the diaries of Lewis and Clark,

Continental maps, construction paper

the ship logs of Captain James Cook, the writings of the historian Herodotus, and the accounts of the travels of Marco Polo.

The whole idea of the inquiry/discovery paradigm is to shift the center of gravity in what it means to be a student. Students are accustomed to working with what are known as "tertiary" materials. Tertiary sources are those which have been processed by others, most commonly into the form of textbooks, workbooks, etc. Such sources are not the kind one searches in for meaning on the basis of one's own investigations. Rather, meaning (at least the kind of meaning the author wishes the reader to find) is presented to the student. This may seem efficient at first glance. Why, after all, waste time allowing adolescents to search for meaning in old diaries, on archaeological digs, or doing complicated projects when it can be given to them in the form of lecture, text reading or problems? While such a question may seem loaded with sarcasm, consider the evidence of how students are typically taught. Without getting into too much detail here, let me assure the reader the research evidence is overwhelming that most of the teaching most of the time in American schools is didactic.

When the shift in the center of gravity of what it means to be a student occurs, three things follow. First, students must take on the responsibility of finding their own answers to difficult questions. John Gardner, former Secretary of Health, once noted that a

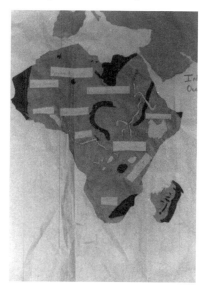

"A grand sight greeted us as we entered this remarkable museum. The magnificent furniture once owned by members of the Russian royal family was so close you could sit in it! We then were shown the icon room. These were religious paintings of saints that they believe are 'windows to the soul.'"

Travis Willson, 6th grade

MARCO POLO

"The roof of the Lord's Great Palace is very lofty and the walls of the palace are all covered with gold and silver. They are also adorned with representations of sculptured and gilt dragons, beasts and birds, and other sundry subjects. The outside of the roof is colored with vermilion, yellow, green, blue, and other hues, which are fixed with a varnish so fine that they shine like crystal and lend a resplendent luster...."

Marco Polo, 1275

fundamental problem of school life is that teachers give students cut flowers when they should be giving them seeds. What he meant by this is that we unwittingly deprive students of both the joy and the responsibility of discovering meaning in learning. We do it by denying them the raw, unprocessed accounts and activities they so desperately need.

Secondly, the business of motivation in learning shifts from being the teacher's responsibility to becoming a shared responsibility of students and teachers. Perhaps you have noticed that it is typical of lesson plans that they have a step in which the teacher is supposed to motivate the class. Why is this so? The answer is someone has sold the teaching profession on the idea that the material to be learned in school needs a teacher/promoter in order to make it palatable. This is generally true in terms of setting the condition for learning. But the fallacy in reasoning is to look to the teacher rather than to the material itself as the answer. No doubt teaching is an art form that calls on complex abilities. But the more we allow the center of gravity to shift to the teacher away from the student the more dependent we make the student, and the more we lessen his/her instincts to find out things without being told.

And thirdly, the conduct of inquiry requires that people work together across disciplinary lines. Most purposeful inquiry/dis-

Asian Jungle Game

covery projects are simply too big for one person. They take teamwork. Good school-based inquiry takes inspired teachers who are willing to work together bringing to the table the best of their disciplines. And the school experiences that are the most inspiring, that build the most lasting memories are those which involve students working together. When the academic curriculum finally realizes what the athletic curriculum, the drama curriculum, and the other extracurricular areas already know about human needs and learning, then progress will be possible. No wonder the intellectual Robert Maynard Hutchins observed more than half a century ago, "Students resort to the extracurricular because the curriculum is so stupid."

Teaching, as Jean Piaget once noted, isn't telling. It is in fact a deeper, more complex art. Piaget thought teachers' genius lay in their ability to organize the environment for learning. Anatole France said it well: "The whole art of teaching is only the art of awakening the natural curiosity of young minds...." The same curiosity, no different in quality at all, is what drove Lewis and Clark to do what they did. It is what summoned young Marco Polo to adventures so far beyond the reach of his wildest dreams as to seem unimaginable even today. And this same curiosity is what drives a teacher to see in a student the possibilities for excellence beyond the student's own wildest hopes and dreams.

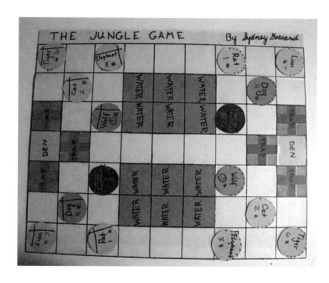

Jungle Game Board, Sydney Gossard, 6th grade

MARCO POLO

Assumptions

All of this is somewhat problematic, of course, because the arguments on behalf of integrated studies are generally based on certain assumptions about the nature of knowledge. To the extent that teachers and others with a vested interest in the curriculum think those arguments are persuasive, the assumptions make sense. Let us examine three such assumptions worthy of consideration.

The first assumption about the nature of knowledge is there is simply too much information to contain it in a school curriculum.

Knowledge is not a scarce resource such as petroleum that could eventually be depleted. Rather, knowledge creates knowledge. There will only be more, not less of it in years to come. Knowledge feeds on itself resulting in geometric rather than linear expansions. Those devoted to complete coverage of subjects in the school curriculum will need to look elsewhere for comfort. There is simply too much to cover. And the overall expansion of knowledge can be applied to individual subjects.

Today a typical supermarket carries two to three hundred periodicals tucked away on some shelves in a corner of the store. The Seattle Public Library, a typical urban repository, offers its

Chinese Block Printing

readers more than 3000 titles of periodicals from which to choose. And so on. No matter how you look at it, the amount of knowledge available from which to build curriculum is out of control. Of course, it never was under control in a dynamic sense, only in an inert sense. So, the thinking goes, traditional attempts at coverage won't work, and some means of combining subject matter is at least one answer to the dilemma. Hence the case for integration.

Selective Coverage

But combining subjects even where it might make sense to do so, an intriguing idea, just isn't enough. There is still too much to cover, especially when one considers that the mere combining of subjects offers no guarantee the combinations arrived at will represent the essential knowledge from the various disciplines selected for integration.

This brings us to the second assumption about the nature of knowledge and integrated studies: selective coverage. Because integrated studies offerings are usually based on themes, they make no pretense about coverage in the traditional sense. Rather the

Journeys Journal Entry

"Neither the weather nor the mountains could stop the armies of Genghis Khan. He started the great Mongolian Empire in the 1300's and it soon became the largest empire in world history. An American scientist believes he knows where the legendary Genghis Khan is buried and he is now in Mongolia trying to find the grave."

David Morris, 7th grade

"While I was sleeping on the roof, I dreamed that I was on the wing of a great bird that was flying with me towards Mecca and then to Yemen. We then flew eastward and thereafter towards the south, then... to finally land in a dark and green country; here it left me. I was astonished at this dream and said to myself, 'If the shaykh can interpret my dream for me, he is all that they say he is.'"

*Ibn Battuta,
1326*

approach is more often oriented toward large ideas that cut across disciplinary boundaries. Mortimer Adler's Great Books program, for example, is based on the writings of hundreds of authors over the centuries, and its focus is on important ideas that have changed the world. Those ideas include justice, power, love, wealth, beauty, etc. The point of the program is that if students are interested in how the idea of, say, citizenship has been developed by great thinkers over time, then they merely need to follow that theme in their studies. And because citizenship is truly a theme not restricted to any one academic discipline, the readings come from science, history, civics, literature, the arts, mathematics, philosophy, religion, economics, etc. As an aside, Adler's program provides a useful adjunct to integrated studies programs because it lends some of the needed intellectual perspective often lacking in activity-oriented integrated studies curricula.

But regardless of the proportional emphasis on a traditional or activity-oriented approach to teaching and learning, integrationists argue the focus on significant ideas or themes offers a way out of the forest of information in which it is becoming increasingly easy to get lost. Thus integrated studies, or at least thematic learning, would appear to have an upper hand in this equation because by definition it should seek the *best points of intersection* among disciplines, and those points are invariably found in the

*Plant and Shells,
watercolor,
Dale Stolmeier,
8th grade*

realm of significant ideas. However, opponents will argue the same procedure can be followed within specific academic disciplines, and that it is not an exclusive feature of integrated studies. Good teachers, it is claimed, have always taught this way, drawing out significant ideas and connecting them to larger patterns. And when this model is expanded to include two or more teachers and subject areas, the potential for significant connections increases.

Transcendent Purposes

The third assumption integrated studies makes about the nature of knowledge is that knowledge should be learned for reasons that transcend the ordinary academic purposes of school life. And here what is essentially at stake is the application of knowledge to true life experience. Anyone who has taken a course in foreign language or educational statistics knows how difficult it is to remember even the basics from the course. Even people who achieved top grades will say things like, "I don't remember much; I just studied for the tests." We should not be surprised when teaching and learning is purely academic in the sense of "learn the material and show that you learned it on the test," that students neither expect to retain nor to use in any practical way what they studied. This is not so much a way of saying that the knowledge

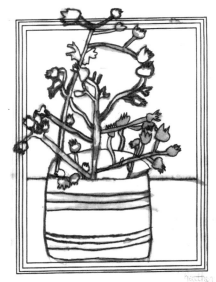

Potted Plant,
watercolor,
Heather White,
7th grade

Journeys
Journal
Entry

"Have you ever wondered where dreams come from? The truth is dreams do not just happen to us. They develop from images we make ourselves. We create our own dreams. They belong to us. No one can tell you what you can or cannot dream. Many famous persons' ideas came from their dreams including Mozart's music and stories by Robert Louis Stevenson...."

Dennis Meyer,
7th grade

IBN BATTUTA

*"I said to Abu Bakr,
'What kind of animals
are these?' He
replied, 'They are
hippopotami that have
come out to pasture
ashore.' They are
bulkier than horses,
have manes and tails,
and their heads are
like horses' heads but
their feet like el-
ephants' feet. I saw
these hippopotami
again when we sailed
down from Timbuktu
to Gao."*

*Ibn Battuta,
1352*

was trivial in the first place, or even that such courses have no value. The reason for the atrophy for most learners may well be that the opportunity to apply the information they "learned" never presented itself. Aristotle noted in his writing that it is in doing that we learn best. His point was that knowledge applied has more staying power.

A common approach to learning in integrated studies is the project method. Projects are things you do, not just information you learn. Much of the current thought in brain research suggests that human beings are "wired" to do projects, that projects are a natural way for us to learn and to get things done. Such an approach to the curriculum and to knowledge inevitably takes students and teachers out into the real world. An example of such an interdisciplinary approach to knowledge is a project done recently by a group of middle school students at James Bay Community School in Victoria, British Columbia who were responsible for the removal of all chlorofluorocarbon-containing styrofoam cups, etc. from the food services of the British Columbia Ferry System and from the Victoria Public Schools. Just imagine the amount of research in different areas students would need to do in order to put a project together that resulted in such dramatic changes in

*Crocodile sketch,
Sterling Hampton,
6th grade*

public policy. Projects have a way of energizing learners with the power of knowledge applied. And to those who question whether all knowledge has direct application to the real world, our answer is no, just as it is no to the question of whether it is reasonable to attempt to integrate every facet of the curriculum. Such questions, however, are rather diversionary when one considers the lost opportunities to make real world applications and to integrate studies where it is reasonable to do so.

The most cogent counterargument to projects as a way to make knowledge meaningful is that school, by definition, is not the real world. It is purposely set aside from real life as a time to acquire the vast reservoirs of knowledge that separate us from other creatures. Attempts to carry out "real life" projects, it is said, destroy the very reason for having school in the first place. Projects are available to us throughout life, even during nonschool hours during the school years, but the opportunity to study academic knowledge in disciplined settings occurs only during the school years. Yes, of course. Our argument is not that everything should be reduced to projects. But we desperately need them as a major strategy.

"What is the difference between a crocodile and an alligator? One difference is that a crocodile has a long, pointed snout and an alligator has a short, blunt one. Another is that a crocodile's teeth always show but the alligator's teeth are not seen when its mouth closes. Crocodiles prefer salt water but alligators live in fresh water."

Sterling Hampton, 6th grade

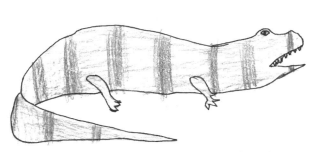

Carribean caiman, Raymond Fitzgerald, 6th grade

The Nature of Reflective Thinking

Sidebars:
The Exploits of Columbus and the Conquistadors

COLUMBUS

"I began sailing at a very early age and have not stopped yet. The art of navigation inspires the navigator to want to know the secrets of the world. God made me proficient in navigation, gave me some knowledge of astronomy, geometry and aritmetic, and endowed me with the ability to draw the sphere, accurately placing cities, rivers, mountains, islands, and harbors."

Christopher Columbus, 13th century

Teachers and students today have access to a variety of active teaching and learning strategies including discovery, inquiry, quality process, simulation, group investigation, and a number of others. These strategies have made it possible to create learning landscapes that are attractive, engaging, and potentially productive. Strategies of engagement have a common property in that they invite learners to share in active experiences. For children and adolescents, experience is the port of entry to reflective thinking. Without experience, students are relegated to a school life of verbal knowledge, which is, as Jean Piaget noted, not real knowledge. But experience alone is an insufficient criterion without some consideration of which experiences are more meaningful than others.

John Dewey addressed the crucial nature of experience in learning when he wrote "... the fundamental fallacy in methods of instruction lies in supposing that experience on the part of pupils may be assumed." Dewey went on to say that "ready-made" subject matter and delivery systems in their variety of artificial forms (textbooks, workbooks, lesson plans, etc.) are a "waste of time." He stated further that experience with ideas should begin in the most concrete forms and that it should be as "unscholastic" as possible. He advised teachers who wished to involve their students in experience "to call to mind the sort of situation that presents itself outside of school." He suggested the most productive areas of endeavor in which to engage students are real problems and social issues, and students should begin their inquiry by trial and error, rather than an academic level. The important thing, he said, is the ultimate quality of a problem to be investigated because good problems "give the pupils something to do, not something to learn and the doing is of such a nature as to demand thinking, or the intentional noting of connections; learning naturally results." So Dewey is saying two things: 1) experience is necessary in learning, and 2) the *quality* of the experience is of great importance.

Dewey was convinced that much of what comprises the official learning environment is "hostile" to reflective thinking, or the analytical processes used to intellectualize experience. He decried the "great premium put upon listening, reading, and the reproduction of what is told and read." No wonder, he stated, when students go to school they might as well leave their minds at home because they can't use their minds in the abstract, unintellectual curriculum that prevails.

John Dewey wrote much of what appears above in the second decade of the twentieth century. So one might suppose things have improved considerably over the past eight decades. In fact, they have at the level of educational theory and in the realms of research in learning and teaching and among a relatively small, seemingly random cadre of informed teachers and administrators. But according to research by John Goodlad, the day-to-day realities of school life have changed very little. Beyond the familiar one teacher, thirty student configuration, he noted the single most predictable event in secondary classrooms is the lecture and in elementary classrooms, seatwork. Both are passive, abstract pursuits that offer little hope of intellectual stimulation. Goodlad wrote: "...three categories of student activity marked by passivity—written work, listening, and preparing for assignments—dominate in the likelihood of their occurring at any given time at all three levels of schooling. The chances are better than 50-50 that if you were to walk into any of the classrooms of our sample, you would see one of these three activities under way...."

William Glasser (1992) writes, "...students in school...are asked to learn well enough to remember for important tests innumerable facts that both they and their teachers know are of no use except to pass the tests." Glasser calls this "throwaway information" because it is unconnected to experience. Glasser goes on to

Journeys
Play
Script

Columbus: But Juan, you know we came here to find China.
Juan: I was excited at first, but after eating that dolphin for breakfast, we are all ready to call it quits. I'm sick of the sea and miss my wife and kids!
Columbus: I'm sorry you feel that way, Juan. How about we go just one more day? If we don't find land, I promise we'll head back.

Amy Kolb,
6th grade

65

COLUMBUS

"I left Granada on Saturday, the 12th day of the month of May in the same year of 1492 and went to the town of Palos, which is a seaport. There I fitted out three vessels, very suited to such an undertaking. I set my course for the Canary Islands.... I decided to write down everything I might do and see and experience on this voyage, from day to day, and very carefully."

Christopher Columbus, 1492

say a majority of students, even good ones, believe much of the present academic curriculum is not worth the effort it takes to learn it. No matter how well teachers manage them, if students do not find quality in what they are asked to do, they will not work hard enough to learn the material.

Learning material in a curriculum of good quality must be heavily invested in meaningful concrete experience. It meets the conditions of what could reasonably be called an experiential focus in teaching and learning. The learning material, while student-centered, is heavily invested in historical content; beyond that, it is informal, exploratory, and interdisciplinary, replete with opportunities for teachers and students to link ideas across subject matter disciplines. We mentioned earlier that engagement strategies are only *potentially* productive. Engaging students actively is only half the battle.

Active student engagement in a meaningful problem or issue makes it possible to create the conditions for reflective thinking because the students are bonded together by a common experience. The experience becomes the focal point of reflective thought. Students reconstruct, evaluate, brief, second-guess, and otherwise mentally reorganize what they did or what they are doing. It is from concrete, common experience that students and teachers together can build the intellectual scaffolding necessary to the creation of ideas or concepts. This is not easy to do.

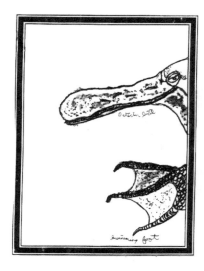

Shoreline bird bill and foot, Mark Swannack, 7th grade

Goodlad said that in his seven-state study he saw virtually no evidence of teachers teaching concepts. He concluded either they felt concepts were unimportant or they themselves do not think conceptually. But concept teaching through reflective thinking is, in fact, the key to the saying "less is more," because a few concepts carefully considered are worth far more as intellectual currency than the great amounts of information students are typically asked to cover. Teachers and learners must deliberately slow down, cover less, and think at length about what they are learning. Jean Rousseau knew this, and that is why he advised teachers to teach less and teach it well. Alfred North Whitehead restated it as, "What you teach, teach thoroughly."

It must be made clear that although it is imperative to include concrete experience as an integral part of student learning, there should be no bias against abstract thought in classrooms. We need it desperately. But the abstract thought we seek must be rooted in a meaningful frame of reference called experience. This is what Francis Bacon meant when he said learning ought to be about facts, but one's own facts and not someone else's. Bacon's Experience>Mind>Meaning model is basically the same as Dewey's.

The role of experience and reflection in learning has been explored at length more recently by cognitive psychologists. Experience and reflection are the twin pillars of significance in

"On Tuesday we made it to Barcelona, one of Spain's major Mediterranean seaports. The Museum of Modern Art was very interesting and had a special exhibit of paintings by Salvador Dali. Viewing Day on the Beach was like entering a dream. Images of round bodies floated through the air like clouds of dull color. I liked it very much."

Andrew Reinertsen, 6th grade

*Time Travel
News Broadcast*

The Exploits of Columbus and the Conquistadors

1. King John II of Portugal
2. Cardinal Gonzalez de Mendoza
3. Doña Isabell Moniz
4. Felipe Moniz
5. Doña Beatriz de Peraza
6. Father Bartoleme de Las Casas
7. Paolo Toscanelli
8. Martin Alonzo Pinzon
9. Vicente Yanez Pinzon
10. Francisco Pinzon
11. Taino Indian children
12. Christopher Columbus
13. King Ferdinand of Spain

14. Queen Isabella of Spain
15. Chief Guacanagari of Cibao
16. Diego de Arana
17. Pedro de Alvarado
18. Captain Diego de Ordaz
19. Melchior
20. Rodrigo de Escobedo
21. Father Juan Diaz
22. Jeronimo de Aguilar
23. Lord Cacamatzin
24. Lord Cuitlahuac
25. Doña Marina
26. Hernando Cortes
27. Aztec Emperor Montezuma II

28. Bernal Diaz del Castillo
29. Xicotenga
30. Olintecle
31. Estephan
32. Father Marcos
33. Alonso Yanez
34. Alvar Lopez
35. Pedro de Creza
36. Gonzalo Pizarro
37. Francisco Pizarro
38. Lord Inca Atahualpa
39. Lord Inca Huascar
40. Francisco de Orellana

New World Journeys of Discovery

MONTEZUMA

"[Doña Marina's] father died while she was still very young, and her mother married another cacique to whom she bore a son. To avoid any impediment, they gave Doña Marina to some Indians from Xicalango by night in order to be unobserved. The whole story seems very much like that of Joseph and his brethren in Egypt. Doña Marina knew the languge of Mexico and she knew the language of Tabasco and Yucatan."

Bernal Díaz del Castillo, 1520

constructivist learning theories. Robert Karplus, the director of Science Curriculum Improvement Study (SCIS), developed a three-phase learning model consisting of preliminary exploration, invention, and discovery. The process was based on Karplus' belief that students need to start by exploring the concept to be learned using concrete materials. By starting an investigation using concrete materials, a learner has a direct experience from which to begin processes of abstract thought. But to be meaningful, the learning cycle must continue beyond the direct experience.

Jerome Bruner makes a clear distinction between learning *by* experience and learning *from* experience, and the distinction lies not so much with the experience itself as with how one reflects back on the experience. Bruner notes that animals typically learn by experience. A dog that burns its paw on the stove will not repeat such a mistake. The dog is too intelligent for that. But the dog is incapable of reflecting on such ideas as heat transfer or thermodynamics as a result of its experience. So experience, valuable as it is, is not enough. Reflective thought must accompany the experience. These are the dual imperatives of concept development. I'm not suggesting that we burn kids' hands or have them put their tongues on bridge railings in freezing weather in order to afford them the opportunity to reflect on the nature of conductivity. But I am suggesting that in order for them to think reflectively about important things we must provide them with direct experience. Furthermore, we must provide opportunities for them to reconstruct their experience. The implication is that a given activity must be extended beyond the experiential phase into a time of reflection.

Time as a Curriculum Variable

This brings up the element of time. John Carroll has suggested that time is the least thoughtfully considered variable in the curriculum. Most of what we expect students to learn in school settings is configured by class periods of an hour or less. This is obviously true at secondary levels where separate subjects are assigned their own time slots, but it is truer than we care to admit at elementary levels. In addition, most subjects are set on time vectors from day one of the school year forward. Teachers feel the need to "keep going" in order to provide the coverage demanded by the textbook. This is particularly true of the "hard" subjects of math, science, English, social studies, etc. It is less true of such "soft" subjects as art, physical education, industrial arts, etc., and that is one reason students prefer those subjects even though they are convinced (we convinced them) they are less important.

Carroll stated that if we slowed the curriculum down for most students they could learn more. His proposition is that the curriculum favors those who learn quickly. The problem, he said in so many words, is that most students never have the opportunity to process or to reflect on what they are learning, so in essence what is taught never gets internalized or connected to other learning. This problem exists whether one is teaching experientially or in more traditional ways. It has been noted that average and below average learners often leave out steps when they try to solve problems. Apparently they go too fast in their efforts to keep up, taking mental short cuts. An example of this would be persons playing, say, checkers who rather impulsively make what seem on the surface to them to be reasonable moves. Often the moves our checker players make are poorly thought-out and could be vastly improved by their talking through a move with another person, in which case certain lapses in logic would be avoided. To those who might think such a procedure in checkers would be unfair, it is well to keep in mind our teaching/learning objective is not to win against an opponent but to become better at what one does.

Robert Sternberg and others have suggested students be encouraged to "think aloud" with a partner in order to slow themselves down. Thinking aloud allows learners to find out how well developed their ideas really are. Thinking aloud brings the process to the surface, giving learners an opportunity to compare and contrast their ideas with those of others.

Piaget wrote about the social knowledge that develops from

STEPHAN

working and interacting with others. He was convinced the linguistic compatibility found within the peer group enables students to teach each other quite effectively, perhaps more effectively than an adult teacher, whose language structure is quite different. And the Russian psychologist, Lev Vygotsky, wrote about the community of knowledge and insight that must be shared by the members of the community in order for learning to come to life.

Strategies can be devised for slowing down our thoughts in order to make them more productive. Imagine a situation of twenty socks in a drawer where there are red socks and white socks in a ratio of three to two. How many socks would you have to take out of the drawer in order to be certain of having a matched pair either red or white? This is a difficult problem for many children partly because it purposely contains some extraneous information. But is the problem inherently difficult or is it difficult because we expect students to solve it with paper and pencil having read it from a page? Imagine two alternate methods of trying to solve the problem: 1) talking about it while drawing diagrams with a partner; and 2) simply reaching into a container that held the socks, several times, and trying to reconstruct with a partner why you got the results you did. Both of these methods take considerably more time than we generally allow for such problems, and both yield better results.

THE TENOCH

Tenochtitlan's Only Daily Pa
Price: 1 flint chip   Flint Knif

Today, Nov. 3, 1519 will be wet in Mexico with a high of 77. find more on B4.	The chocolate price jump sky high, due to a flood in south Mexico, C1.	The Pumas get smashed by the panthers. D5

Some teachers, apparently satisfied with the results we are getting, simply do not see how we could possibly slow the curriculum down. There is, after all, a great deal of information to cover and much to tell the students. One possible means of accommodation is for teachers to talk less. Research shows that teachers outtalk their students by a ratio of three to one. Since students outnumber teachers about twenty-seven to one you don't have to be a mathematics major to figure out that students are allowed very little time to think aloud. A remedy for this situation, of course, is cooperative learning of some sort where students are expected to share their thoughts and to listen to the thoughts of others. Cooperative learning changes not only the amount of student-to-student interaction so desperately needed for reflective thinking to occur, it also changes the very social fabric of classrooms. Students are given far more control over their time, and teachers are able to shift from teaching as telling to allowing learning to take place.

Now much of this is already common knowledge to those informed and dedicated teachers who attempt to stay abreast of events in their field. The problem lies with their many colleagues who are less informed about how to create the proper conditions for learning. But even among those who promote inquiry, problem solving, etc. there is a reluctance to build in the extra time

Journeys
News Report

"Market Thief Apprehended
A 20 year-old man trying to steal fresh corn at the Tlateloco Market yesterday afternoon was captured by nearby sellers of obsidian swords. The thief had started to run down the aisles where produce of all kinds was being sold and he was found to have a quantity of sunflowers and chiles in a basket he was carrying."

Jeff McLean,
6th grade

TLAN TABLOID

Hail King Montezuma!!

Month of Feather Banners (November, 1519)

Tenaochtitlan troubles - At approximately

1'o clock. an army of 400 fierce beasts approached the town of Tenaóchtitlan. The height of these terrible creatures is two times the size of a regular man and quite longer. This

ACAHUALPA

"What I shall tell will be as an eyewitness and as a man to whom God chose to give a part in such a strange and hitherto never experienced voyage of discovery. ...[C]aptain Orellana picked out fifty-seven men with whom he embarked in the boat and in certain canoes. He began to proceed down this river [Amazon] with the idea of promptly turning back if food was found which turned out just the reverse of what we all expected."

*Father Gaspar de Carvajal,
1542*

needed for genuine reflection by students and teachers. Such a need is obviously not perceived by school as being necessary for teachers, who have little or no time to reflect either alone or with fellow teachers; therefore it is little wonder that teachers often neglect to build in reflective thinking time with their students.

From Teaching to Learning

The economist Peter Drucker states, in his provocative book, *The New Realities*, that schools will never improve until classrooms become places where people have crossed the frontier from teaching to learning. When the focus in a classroom is on teaching, a teacher-centered curriculum results. Teacher-centered instruction is the stuff of lesson plans, scripted activities, behavioral objectives, and predictable outcomes. When the focus in a classroom is on learning, a student-centered curriculum results. Student-centered learning allows learners the latitude to make choices, to play to their strengths, to work at length on projects, to develop ideas, to cooperate with other students, and to reflect on the quality of their work. Remember, teaching is a means to an end called learning.

Instances of crossing the frontier from teaching to learning abound, but rarely in classrooms. They are found, rather, in the

real world where learners make their own connections, do their own investigations, and continuously process what they are learning. A computer-literate acquaintance was recently asked how she had learned so much about computers. She replied that she had learned what she knew by hanging around, using computers, and talking to other interested people. She said that when she was in high school, there was a computer hooked up through a terminal to a mainframe and she used to go down to the little room where it was housed, close the door, get on line, and that was the beginning. People didn't even know she was there. She said he had never taken a computer class. Perhaps you could cite similar experiences in real learning from your own experience. The point is we should reflect on these examples because they have the power to redirect our sense of teaching and learning away from formal books and test-oriented procedures to the creation of learning environments that approximate real world learning.

One other condition essential to the establishment of classrooms where students and teachers think reflectively is that of a healthy emotional/intellectual landscape. Not long ago we observed in a third grade class where the teacher was doing an inquiry social studies lesson. The approach was inductive, there were artifacts for the students to examine, the students were working in teams, and they were encouraged to make inferences from their obser-

"The Brazilian giant otter (Pteronura brasiliensis) *is truly a giant with some reaching the amazing length of 7 feet! This creature is diurnal, active in the day, and has very good vision for hunting. It eats mostly fish and crabs, one of its favorites being the black pataka. They are endangered now and are a rare sight. It would hurt the Amazon ecosystem if they become extinct, just like any other animal."*

Kristi Freese,
6th grade

Leopard and Giant Otter, linoleum prints, Kristi Freese, 6th grade

ATAHUALPA

"Cicero called writing the witness of time, the teacher of life, the light of truth. I only ask that my work be kindly regarded for I feel it is offered in truth. I decided to write about the Incas for my own enjoyment and to avoid the consequences of idleness. To better come to the truth, I went to Cuzco where I met Cayu Tupac, the one living descendant of the Lord Inca Huayna Capac."

Pedro de Cieza
de León,
16th century

vations and recordings. This was all to the good. Unfortunately, the atmosphere was tense and rigid. The teacher kept interrupting the students to remind them to behave even though there was no evidence of misbehavior. Additionally, it became clear that the teacher was looking for "right" answers, and the students found themselves trying to please her or second-guess her wishes. None of the spontaneity that Piaget said must be present was there. Risk taking, outlandish ideas, a sense of humor, a relaxed and friendly pace, all were lacking. In this case, we had what appeared to be a good formal curriculum being unraveled by a bad hidden curriculum.

The proper conditions for reflective thinking derive from a complex set of strategies developed by the teacher. Learning by doing is simply not sufficient of itself; neither is direct experience although both are important. The teacher must be a guide, a fellow inquirer, an organizer of the environment, and a mediator of students' thinking. The teacher must establish a new set of priorities that run counter to the prevailing modes of instruction and classroom management. The teacher must be committed to increasing the amount of student-to-student interaction, the number of decisions made by students, the amount of time given to reconstructing learning experiences, and the freedom given to students to speak their mind and to take intellectual and emotional risks. When these conditions are met, the term "paradigm shift" moves beyond the realm of cliche and into the realm of reality.

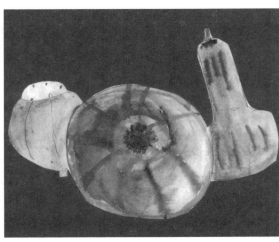

Native South American Vegetables, watercolor, Ben Fredricks, 7th grade

VI

Integration and Academic Integrity

Sidebars:
Elizabeth I and the Explorations of Drake and Raleigh

"There is a general vengeance which secretly pursues wrongdoers and suffers them not to prosper... When the great and mighty injure their inferiors it seems unwise for their own safety and rest. For Aesop teaches that even the ant is not without her anger and even an eagle laying her eggs high in Jupiter's lap cannot escape the payment of wrong done to the insect."

Francis Drake, 16th century

Interdisciplinary curriculum means curriculum that combines and somehow integrates two or more typically separate disciplines. Obviously, in order to accomplish this some accommodations must be made. This is true because school subjects are typically taught in isolation in spite of all the talk about interdisciplinary approaches to teaching and learning. When a subject, say mathematics or English, is taught in isolation, a teacher and his or her students can give that subject complete attention. The subject itself is the focus of attention. It becomes an end in itself rather than a means to some other end. On the other hand, when two or more subjects are combined, the focus changes, however subtly. More time is spent trying to explore and act on the possible relationships between the subjects. The relationship is often established by identifying a common theme to which each of the disciplines can make some meaningful contribution. Such a theme might be "Invention," "Exploration," "Discovery," "Environment," etc. Thus the idea of the theme becomes the end and the contributing disciplines become means toward that end.

This is not to say a given teacher teaching one subject might not attempt to relate that subject to other areas of life. But that is what we would call an isolated random effect. One teacher tries to establish connections and another does not. When teachers consciously try to teach more than one subject together, the attempt to make connections, at least from one subject to another, is no longer a random effect, but a planned effect. This logic follows for students as well, depending on whether they study subjects alone or study them together.

Teachers, students, parents, and others who have something at stake in the educational enterprise must be convinced that the needed accommodations in the traditional structure of separately-taught disciplines is worthwhile. This is not always an easy task, and the challenge of doing it well should not be underestimated. People have every right to question a break with the traditional, discipline-centered curriculum and its replacement with an inter-disciplinary, thematically oriented approach to the curriculum. In fact, the arguments for keeping subjects separated are often compelling. It is important to keep in mind that not everything can or should be integrated. The judgments of what to integrate and what to leave to separate account are the judgments that teachers need to make wisely and with discernment. Just as it is often patently artificial to separate children's learning experiences into academic disciplines that may make sense to the advanced scholar but not to the child, so too, is there a very real danger that accompanies the tyranny of forced integration.

What happens to learning when students are taught separate subjects, out of context with and unrelated to one another? As we noted above, sometimes it is necessary to do so, but far more often the failure to integrate knowledge leads to a failure of the promise of a liberal education to become a reality. The purpose of school is more about citizenship, participation, and a desire to learn than it is about the so-called mastery of separate subjects. It is during these years of emergence from childhood that students begin to glimpse the possibilities of scholarship, but more often their immediate interests run to friendships, projects, and activities.

These interests are frequently treated as problems that get in the way of learning. This is all the more the case to the extent that school learning consists mainly, as John Goodlad has observed, of teacher talk and what is euphemistically called seatwork. This is not an argument for school merely as a place of social gathering or as a place where students do whatever they choose. Rather, it is an attempt to say that cooperative activities, group projects, and school as places where citizenship, participation, and esprit de corps occur are at the heart of the curriculum. These are far more likely to ignite the spark of learning than are the contrived, expert-oriented, narrow confines of separate subjects, which diminish not only academic connections but the connections among

Journeys Play Script

Jim: I can't remember the Spanish word for "dinner."

Amy: I don't know it either but we can use sign language.

Jim: Wait, that looks like a restaurant over there.

Larissa: Come on, let's go inside and find out.

Amy: Wow, this place is nice; the owner must be well-off. Most Peruvians are poor and 3/5 can't read or write.

Jim: Someone said there is little government aid for the needy so lots of kids live on the streets in cities here....

Larissa Leifer, 6th grade

"The Cimaroons have a town near a fair river on the side of a hill... forty-five [leagues] from Panama. There is a great tree midway from which we might at once discern the North Sea and the South. In that great tree they had cut steps to ascend to the top where they also made a bower so ten or twelve might easily sit. From here one might without any difficulty plainly see the Atlantic Ocean and the South Sea."

Francis Drake, 1573

80

teachers as well. One of the great ironies of school life is that we expect students to put the various curricular pieces together into something called a liberal education when teachers themselves make no claim to having done it. We expect students to emerge from our schools with a sense of citizenship when the faculty itself seldom works together, which could serve as a model of citizenship. A useful principle to keep in mind is that the logical consequence of the separation of faculty from each other and the deliberate separation of subjects from each other is a fragmented sense of knowledge and of self among learners. When teachers work in isolation, when subjects are taught in isolation, why should we not expect *students* to view learning as fragmented? And why should they themselves not feel isolated?

Limitations of the Interdisciplinary Approach to Curriculum

The primary purpose of this work is to examine the virtues of the interdisciplinary approach to curriculum. But like anything else, no matter how beneficial, it can be both overdrawn and misapplied. Two of the potentially most damaging applications of interdisciplinary curriculum are 1) the siren call of superficiality, and 2) the temptation to use it when a separate subjects approach

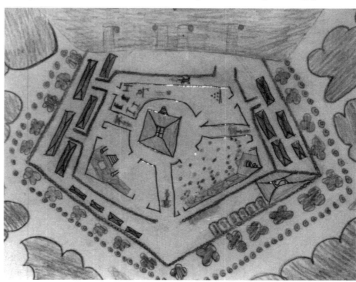

Drake's Port Pheasant Derek Miller, 6th grade

would serve both teachers and students better. Let us look at each of these problems in turn.

Among traditionalists and subject matter specialists there is great reluctance to abandon the teaching of important subjects separately. This is so because they fear that mathematics, literature, history, etc., will be watered down and treated superficially in an attempt to meet the compromising demands of some central theme around which an interdisciplinary unit is typically organized. There is the accompanying concern that the orderly progression of knowledge and skills that can be taught when a subject is treated as a curriculum in and of itself will be lost in a random, patchwork attempt to relate it to the particular theme. Finally what one is left with, the critics note, is a shallow, disorganized treatment of mathematics or literature, or some other subject, lacking both depth and continuity. Thus the integrity of a typical mathematics concept such as "measurement" is sacrificed in order to meet the demands of a theme such as "community helpers." Or the beauty and symmetry of a poem such as "Paul Revere's Ride" is misused as an example of an interdisciplinary theme of Transportation. Because of the focus on the organizing theme in a typical interdisciplinary unit, a subject that could be treated in depth as an end in itself becomes merely a means to another end. And where this is so, the subject itself is susceptible

"The native people of Central America belong to many different tribes. One of the most interesting to me are the Maya who live in Guatemala, El Salvador, and the southwestern part of Mexico. Their ancestors build amazing buildings which still stand in the jungle after 1500 years. I wonder if our buildings will last that long?"

Yolanda Howard, 7th grade

Classroom Treehouse

"We were somewhat northward of that cape of [South] America where we departed the strait into the sea.... The winds were such as if all the clouds under heaven had been called together to lay their force upon one place. The seas were rolled up from the depths, even from the roots of the rocks, like a scroll of parchment and being aloft were carried as drifts of snow to water the tops of lofty mountains."

Francis Drake, 1577

to superficial, random treatment. The temptation to consider academic subjects from a purely utilitarian point of view (that is, how well do they fit a particular theme) can lead to such disasters as lower test scores, lessened exposure to the possibilities of a particular subject, and the dominance of some curricular areas, such as social studies, over others, such as mathematics.

The other related problem, that of doing interdisciplinary curriculum when a separate subjects approach might well be superior, is just as vexing. This is an issue which teachers must address carefully. The question should be tied to the curricular goal structure. What are the important things that students must study, and how should they study them? Of course, there is no predictable answer to such a question because local circumstances must always be taken into account. The important thing is not to assume the inherent superiority of one approach over another but to think through the implications for student learning. The only useful answer to this question is to consider carefully the implications of combining subjects over keeping them apart. We should search for meaningful ways in which to integrate learning toward some sense of the seamless whole, but we should never assume that integration is the only answer. In other words, the burden of proof should lie with integration, and not the other way around.

The temptations to integrate subjects or to keep them separate can be avoided by answering a simple question: What is best for students? In other words, decisions made with reference not to an abstract policy that favors separation or integration of subject matter, but with reference to contextual matters such as the development of citizenship, morality, knowledge, and self-realization, would be the best decisions. One can only conclude that sometimes the best answer is integration and sometimes it is separation of subject matter.

The Interdisciplinary Experience and the Preservation of Academic Integrity

Let us turn our attention to a practical application of interdisciplinary curriculum and the question of preserving academic integrity. It is typically the case that interdisciplinary efforts are centered on an organizing theme. Any theme chosen by teachers and students must have sustaining value, and it must be rich in its potential to include the various academic disciplines as meaningful contributors. Thus the choice of themes must be based on some strategic vision of what students need to learn and the ways in which they might learn. In other words, a strategic vision is based not on some set of outcomes agreed upon in advance on behalf of students, but upon the potential for a course of study to be complex in its possibilities for student choices, initiative, teacher and student collaboration, projects, and substantive meaning.

We will take the position that interdisciplinary themes should be selected by teachers and not by students. This is so for two reasons. First of all, teachers themselves must be interested in a topic, and they must be convinced that it has the potential to provide a range of experiences that meaningfully incorporate the various contributing subject matter areas. This is not such a simple matter. But if teachers are not convinced of the contributory potential of a theme, they certainly will not be able to convince their students of its value. Secondly, as teachers we have a responsibility to make decisions about what knowledge is of most worth for the young while keeping in mind that most worthwhile knowledge contains a wide array of possible choices for student learning. Thus students are provided with a structure of agreed upon content, while at the same time they are given the opportunity to find themselves within it. This is the strategic balance between anarchy and authoritarianism in a course of study. It is called democracy.

An example of such a theme is Exploration. Of course, there are many other themes equally rich in possibilities, but Exploration will do for purposes of illustration. Exploration as a theme takes us to the frontier of ideas as they were developed and explored in the arts, sciences, mathematics, literature, and geography. In the Journeys of Discovery curriculum for middle school students, the idea of Exploration becomes not merely a vehicle for identifying meaningful content but a metaphor for the entire process of teaching and learning. The journeys of Herodotus,

Journeys
Journal
Entry

"The worst storm I ever experienced was when the dust blew so thick that they would not let the buses leave school and we had to stay inside for several hours. I remember that it was so dark outside even in the afternoon that the streetlights came on. It was like we were living on another planet...."

*Amber Harris,
7th grade*

W. RALEIGH

"On both sides of the river, we passed the most beautiful country that my eyes ever beheld. We beheld plains of grasses short and green, and groves of trees, as if they had been by all the art and labor in the world so made of purpose. We saw in it strange fish... but for alligators it exceeded, and the people call for the abundance of them the 'river of alligators,' in their language."

Walter Raleigh, 1595

Marco Polo, James Cook, and Lewis and Clark serve to personify their quest through the diaries and accounts of these explorers, thus giving the course of study a human scale which removes it from the abstract, coverage-centered accounts found in typical textbooks.

Once a theme appears to have rich curricular potential, the next step is to seriously consider the possibilities for the various subject matter areas of the curriculum to contribute to the theme. This alone distinguishes interdisciplinary efforts from the separate subjects approach. This is so because teachers will have to collaborate, with each teacher taking the lead in showing how one's discipline can best contribute. A kind of synergy flows from such deliberations, at least when things go well. Teachers will have to model cooperative efforts in order to move the planning stages forward. They will have to practice the same kinds of give-and-take that one hopes students themselves will experience when the curriculum is realized in classroom life. These experiences in themselves represent exploration in the finest sense of the word.

Obviously, a theme such as Exploration is filled with geographic and historical potential. But it quickly extends as well into literature in the form of narrative and epic accounts of adventure. Anyone interested in "exploring" the possibilities that the contributions mathematics might bring to the theme of Exploration discovers the applications of measurement, scale, distance, estimation (for example, Columbus' estimation of the earth's circumference was not nearly so accurate as that derived by those early geometers, the ancient Greeks), time, etc. The science curriculum offers the central skills of science, such as observing, recording, classifying, and verifying in addition to the study of technological advances that have made continued exploration possible throughout the ages. And so on. Themes such as Exploration are in fact so rich in academic curricular potential that the problem becomes not whether disciplines can contribute to the course of study, but how to parcel out the contributions from one grade level to the next in some useful sequence.

The Spiral Curriculum

One of the more liberating ideas in the annals of curriculum development is the concept of the spiral curriculum. In essence, the spiral curriculum is based on the premise that it is crucial to identify those key concepts, skills, and values that students should experience and to teach them each year at increasing levels of sophistication. This allows teachers to choose a stable core of important ideas and to teach them every year while varying the content through which they come to life. Such a perception changes the curriculum experience from the misleading idea of mastery to the reality that learning is more a journey than a point of arrival. By changing the content of what is taught while retaining the core values, concepts, and skills, teachers give students the opportunity to visit and revisit life's important themes. This is the beginning of meaningful learning.

When a matrix of important concepts, skills, and values is established, a curriculum is less susceptible to randomness and the "jumping around" so often associated with interdisciplinary thematic teaching and learning. Thus a question that should be posed before the identification of topics and themes is, "What are the most important concepts, skills, and values that each subject matter area can contribute to student learning?" This question can and should be posed independently of the themes and topics chosen for study. It is the single best guarantee that the curriculum will not become frivolous, skipping superficially from one theme to the next, nor imbalanced in favor of one or two subject areas over others. These are two of the most pressing criticisms of interdisciplinary curriculum, and often the criticisms are right on the mark.

Journeys Journal Entry

"The native bunchgrass we saw is highly nutritious and for many centuries supported vast herds of bison, deer, and other wildlife. The grass has deep roots and kept the land from eroding. Now it has been joined by an invader called cheatgrass which is not good for livestock and difficult to prevent from spreading...."

*Hillary Holmes,
8th grade*

VII

The Importance of Themes

Sidebars:
The Voyages of James Cook and Alexander Mackenzie

"We had no sooner come to an anchor in Royal Bay (Tahiti) than a great number of the natives in their canoes came off to the ship.... Rules to be observed by every person in or belonging to His Majesty's Bark the Endeavor: *By every fair means to cultivate a friendship with the natives, and to treat them with all imaginable humanity."*

James Cook, 1769

A crucial ingredient in interdisciplinary teaching and learning is the idea of thematic focus. A well-chosen theme energizes and directs the conduct of inquiry by teachers and students along the most potentially fruitful paths. There is nothing inherently magic about a unifying theme. It can't rescue poor teaching, for example. But for those interested in the serious pursuit of learning, a thoughtfully selected theme provides a conceptual hub around which activities radiate like spokes on a finely crafted wheel.

A good theme is conceptual in that it represents an idea that transcends time and space. A good theme deepens the level of learning because it serves as a constant reminder that the goal of education is found not in information and skills, but in ideas and values. Information and skills are surely important, but they are not the strategic goal of learning. They are of necessity things that should happen along the way. When they become the end result of learning, training, not education takes place.

Let us take some time to consider a number of themes that have the potential to contribute to environments that are truly educational in nature. These carefully selected themes are representative of key organizing concepts from various disciplines. Mainly, they are themes identified by such professional associations as the National Science Teachers Association (NSTA), the National Council of Teachers of Mathematics (NCTM), The National Council for the Social Studies (NCSS), and the National Council of Teachers of English (NCTE).

First it is useful to consider a goal structure in which such themes might be arranged. While any number of themes may be quite interesting and potentially worthwhile, they take on meaning only when they are set within a larger sense of purpose. Thus the role a goal structure serves is to allow us the luxury of thinking about what we want to accomplish strategically before we delve into things on a tactical, day-by-day basis. An example of such a goal structure is shown below.

Curricula Goal Structure*

1. **The Nature of Science:** the scientific worldview; scientific inquiry; the scientific enterprise.
2. **The Nature of Mathematics:** features of mathematics; mathematical processes.
3. **The Nature of Technology:** science and technology; principles of technology; technology and society.
4. **The Physical Setting:** the universe; the earth; forces that shape the earth; the structure of matter; transformations of energy; the motion of things; the forces of nature.
5. **The Living Environment:** diversity of life; heredity; cells, interdependence of life; flow of matter and energy; evolution of life.
6. **The Human Organism:** human identity; life cycle; basic functions; learning; physical health; mental health.
7. **Human Society:** cultural effects on behavior; group organization and behavior; social change; social trade-offs; forms of political and economic organization; social conflict; worldwide social systems.
8. **The Designed World:** the human presence; agriculture; materials; manufacturing; energy sources; energy use; communication; information processing; health technology.
9. **The Mathematical World:** numbers; symbolic relationships; shapes, uncertainty; summarizing data; sampling; reasoning.

* Adapted from "Goals of Science for All Americans," in J. Rutherford and A. Ahlgren, *Science for All Americans* (1992), Oxford University Press.

cpt. cook

"The situation of few parts of the world are better determined than these islands are, being settled by some hundreds of observations of the sun and moon, and one of the transit of Mercury made by Mr. Green, who was sent out by the Royal Society to observed the transit of Venus."

James Cook, 1769

10. *Historical Perspectives:* displacing the earth from the center of the universe; uniting the heavens and earth; uniting matter and energy, time and space; extending time; setting the earth's surface in motion; understanding fire; splitting the atom; explaining the diversity of life; discovering germs; harnessing power.

11. *Common Themes:* systems; models; constancy; patterns of change; evolution; scale.

12. *Habits of Mind:* values and attitudes; skills.

These goals give us an exemplar. There could be others, but this set of goals will do for our purposes here. Ideally, a team of teachers would modify them, add to them to suit their own priorities, or come up with a different list. Thus, if a group of teachers should decide that "patterns of change" is an idea to be developed in the curriculum, then the themes selected and the day-to-day content should reflect that commitment. One could say the same of "group organization and behavior," "symbolic relationships," or any of the other elements of the goal structure.

It is reasonable to ask where a goal structure comes from or on what basis one should be developed. Rutherford and Ahlgren argue that five criteria ought to form the foundation of a selected goal structure. They state that in particular, concepts should be "chosen that could serve as a lasting foundation on which to build

*Palm Trees and Sun, colored pencil
Melinda Pierce,
6th grade*

more knowledge over a lifetime. The choices then had to meet important criteria having to do with human life and with the broad goals that justify universal public education in a free society." On that basis, they selected utility, social responsibility, the intrinsic value of knowledge, philosophical value, and childhood enrichment as their criteria. Again, one could argue these choices, but they seem to be at the very least a significant place to begin thinking about the purpose of school-based education. Let us see more concretely what they mean by these five criteria posed as a set of questions:

Criteria for Selecting Content

Utility. Will the proposed content—knowledge or skills—significantly enhance the graduate's long-term employment prospects? Will it be useful in making personal decisions?

Social Responsibilty. Is the proposed content likely to help citizens participate intelligently in making social and political decisions on matters involving science and technology?

The Intrinsic Value of Knowledge. Does the proposed content present aspects of science, mathematics, and technology that are so important in human history or so pervasive in our culture that a general education would be incomplete without them?

Tahitian
Sunset,
cut
colored
paper,
Kayla
Leifer,
6th grade

cpt. cook

"In the evening the yawl returned from fishing, having caught two sting rays weighing near 600 pounds. The great quantity of plants Mr. Banks and Dr. Solander found in this place occasioned giving it the name Botany Bay."

James Cook, 1770

Philosophical Value. Does the proposed content contribute to the ability of people to ponder the enduring questions of human meaning such as life and death, perception and reality, the individual good versus the collective welfare, certainty and doubt?

Childhood Enrichment. Will the proposed content enhance childhood (a time of life that is important in its own right and not solely for what it may lead to in later life)?

Rutherford and Ahlgren write, "The schools do not need to be asked to teach more and more content, but to teach less in order to teach it better. By concentrating on fewer topics, teachers can introduce ideas gradually, in a variety of contexts, reinforcing and extending them as students mature. Students will end up with richer insights and deeper understandings than they could hope to gain from a superficial exposure to more topics than they can assimilate."

Thus two ideas emerge as a result of a serious consideration of thematic teaching. The first is that topic selection is or ought to be a strategic decision by teachers who are interested in curriculum development. This removes the focus from the traditional mentality of covering a designated number of credits or subjects as a means of constituting a curriculum. The issue becomes not coverage but selection. Thus the focusing question is "what topics have the most potential for the personal, practical, social, and intellectual development of students?"

The second idea is that we should actually be trying to reduce the range of topics that we teach. On the surface this flies in the face of what we know about the knowledge explosion, that is, that there is so much more knowledge to be learned than there was in the past. But this is true only when one focuses his or her attention at the level of information. True knowledge is always made up of ideas, connections, and attitudes toward learning. To confuse this with seemingly disconnected facts, unrelated skills, dates, and other often discrete forms of information is to miss the point of teaching and learning in a day and age in which no one could reasonably hope to "cover" everything.

The search for significant common themes is at the heart of interdisciplinary studies. The themes, once established, become the rallying point of the curriculum, the place you go when you want to be sure that the pursuit is meaningful and excellent. Themes provide a means for the various contributing disciplines to be at once different, showcasing their unique properties, while at the same time carrying out a similarity of conceptual purpose. The liberating sense of a carefully chosen, content enriching theme is that it is supportive of connected, integrated experiences across the disciplines, and it prohibits a superficial tyranny of integration for its own sake from taking over the curriculum.

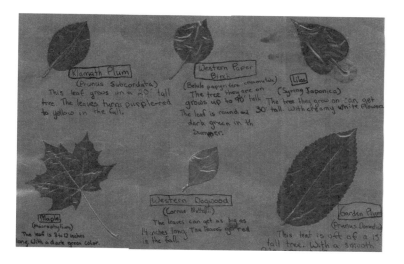

"We traveled toward a stand of low trees we saw in the distance that began to resemble a mysterious grove the closer we went. The bus could only get within a hundred yards so we set off to explore this place on foot. After entering a heavy thicket we emerged on the other side to find tall trees which I identified as oak, willow, cottonwood, and poplar. We also saw many signs of wildlife...."

Scott Hall,
8th grade

Journeys of Discovery
Themes

Sidebars:
The Narratives of Smith, Hutchison, and Bradford

"We went to discover the head of the river and passed many small habitations. In six days we arrived at a town called Powhatan, consisting of some twelve houses, pleasantly seated on a hill. Before are three fertile islands and many cornfields. The prince of this place is called Powhatan, and his people Powhatans."

John Smith,
1624

The Journeys of Discovery curriculum is based on eight broad themes which are encountered and revisited in spiral fashion at gradually increasing levels of sophistication and complexity. The themes, in order to qualify, must meet several important tests. First of all, are the themes truly conceptual —that is, are they representative of ideas that transcend place and time? If so, do they have the potential for transfer and utility beyond the bounds of modes, that is, knowledge received, knowledge discovered, and knowledge constructed? If so, then the themes are suited to knowledge acquisition, cultural literacy, problem solving, experiential learning, and constructivist thinking and doing. Thirdly, we ask whether the themes are fundamentally worth pursuing in each of the separate content areas: the sciences, arts, humanities, social sciences, and mathematics. If so, then the integrity of the curriculum can be ensured. After all, if a theme cannot be pursued within any given discipline, then it is not actually interdisciplinary but in fact peculiar to certain subject matter. And fourthly, we ask whether the themes have the potential to enrich the curriculum and therefore the lives of students and teachers. In order to meet this stringent criterion, there are the tests of utility, aesthetics, truth, and morality. If they meet those tests, then the themes are useful, they are beautiful, they are truthful, and they address an underlying sense of moral goodness.

The fact is that there are many interesting and possibly worthwhile themes from which one could begin to integrate the curriculum. By applying this four-fold test one is able to reduce the list to manageable, meaningful proportions. We do not mean to suggest that we have developed the one magic list, but we can defend our themes on a number of grounds, and that is the important issue whatever themes are chosen. Following is an overview of the Journeys of Discovery themes.

Cause and Effect

Children and adults, amateurs and professionals alike notice effects all around them. Any given effect assumes one or more causes. Leaves fall from the trees in October. Someone is in a happy mood. War breaks out in a region of the world. People speak the same language but with different accents. These are all outcomes, that is to say they are the effects of certain causes. How do things come to be the way they are? Why do things sometimes turn out differently from the way we had hoped they would? What are the causative agents? How can we know? It seems to be in our nature to want to identify the cause or causes of the effects we perceive. What were the major causes of the Civil War? Why did the cake taste differently this time when I thought I followed the same recipe? What were the lasting effects of Lewis and Clark's epic trek to the West?

Sometimes we use rational explanations to determine cause and effect relationships; sometimes we use other means. Always the linkage between cause and effect is explanation. But an explanation is only as good as our information. And our information is only as good as our ability to apply insight to it; otherwise, it's just information. Investigation, experience, and reflection are among the most useful tools in the search for explanation. History, science, literature, religion, the arts, myth, and folk wisdom all take their place as explainers in the search for cause and effect. It is seldom a simple process. More often than not causes are both multiple and complex, especially about real world issues. And just as causes are usually multiple, so are effects. Often, an effect causes another to happen. At some point, teachers and students must acquire a high tolerance for ambiguity. Effects, like causes, are not necessarily what they appear to be. The role of individual or group perception looms large in this business. Astronomy started out as a serious cause and effect "science." The idea held

"Individual months were named by something associated with them like tree leaves turning color. March, for example, was Yah-te-tahl, meaning 'Beginning of Flower Blossoming,' and July was Khoy-tsal, 'Season of the Blue Back (salmon) Run.'"

Brian Gfeller, 8th grade

John Smith

"A great fire was made in a longhouse and a mat spread on one side. A great grim fellow came in painted all over in coal with many snakes and weasel skins stuffed with moss...."

John Smith, 1624

by the ancients (and by many who take astrology seriously today) was that the movement and placement of the stars has serious effects on our daily lives and fortunes.

Commonality and Diversity

One of the hallmarks of investigation is the attempt to document similarities and differences. We ask ourselves, "How am I like my parents and how am I different from them? We explore the similarities and differences between the travels of Marco Polo and those of Francis Drake. We ask why algebra and geometry are so different if they are both branches of mathematics. A teacher asks how students studying such related material at school can be so different in their learning preferences and learning styles. We ask how history and historical fiction are as different as a factual and make-believe account of something while at the same time both can move us nearer to the truth about the past.

Three of the most basic processes of the arts and sciences are at the heart of an exploration of commonality and diversity. Observation, description, and classification are excellent points of departure. Young children notice differences and similarities in the patterns and shapes of leaves. Flowers are alike and different beginning with simple and composite blossoms. Foods fit into different groups. Paintings can be classified by schools, time peri-

Herpetology Presentation

ods, and means of expression. Separate subjects or disciplines arose over time because enough perceived difference developed between and among them. Interdisciplinary teaching and learning turns the equation around and asks what are the similarities?

We observe how things are alike and different. We begin to describe those properties through drawings, words, diagrams, equations, and other means. Classifications emerge on the basis of our observations and descriptions. In time, taxonomies are built. In the 18th century, the Swedish scientist Linneaus developed whole taxonomies for plants and animals based on differences and similarities. He began with a binomial classification that sorted living things into the kingdoms of plants and animals. From there, the classifications were refined into phyla, families, orders, varieties, and so on. Such a taxonomy allows us to categorize a humming bird and a bumblebee as being both alike and different. We tend to classify paintings according to such different schools as realism, impressionism, cubism, surrealism, and so on. Thus Leonardo DaVinci's "Mona Lisa" and Pablo Picasso's "Guernica" are both alike and different.

Systems and Patterns

Children learn early in their lives to think and feel in terms of the patterns of holidays, birthdays, and special events in their lives.

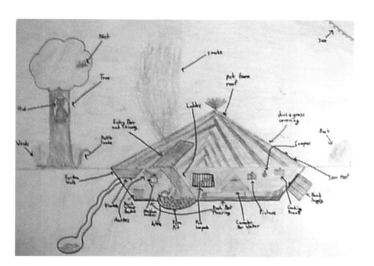

Indian Pit House diagram, Katie Corder, 6th grade

"The Indians of our area made various kinds of houses with the two most common types called the subterranean pithouse and the tulemat lodge. The pithouse was circular and dug to a depth of about four or five feet. A pole frame formed a cone-shaped roof supported by a main beam in the middle near a centrally located fire pit. These homes were usually located on the north side of the river to take advantage of the sunshine and were very energy efficient."

Jason Siler,
7th grade

"They began now to gather in the small harvest they had, and to fit up their houses and dwellings against winter.... Besides waterfowl there was a great store of wild turkeys, besides venison, etc. They had about a peck of meal a week to a person, or now since harvest, Indian corn to that proportion."

William Bradford 1621

They intuitively perceive a system of special days and times of the year which take on a rhythm. The start of school in the fall, Halloween, Thanksgiving, Christmas, Valentine's Day, spring break, and summer vacation all are touch points in the elaborate system of childhood. As students grow older, they may identify with the patterns of the sports calendar of the school: football, followed by basketball, etc. For teachers, the system is often divided into reporting periods of three or four per school year. Units of study begin and culminate following a pattern. The school itself is a complex social/academic system complete with roles, expectations, rules, checkpoints, diplomas, and so on.

The earth, part of the solar system, is itself a system of water, land, creatures, plants, and atmosphere. Our earth system has an established pattern of seasons, with a time to sow and a time to harvest, a time to work and a time to rest. Within families, patterns of behavior and traditions are established complete with histories and mythologies. People search for patterns in their ancestry. Geneticists look for patterns in the work of such scientific undertakings as the human genome project, an intricate system with certain valences that place it in a family of similar elements. Patterns of courage and decency, treachery and deceit, emerge from the pages of literature and history. Art and music are the continuous assembling and reassembling of pigment or notes into new or varied patterns of expression. When a pattern is broken, a whole new field of expression emerges, for example, in the nineteenth century shift from landscape and portrait painting to impressionism. Paradigm shifts in science represent fundamental reappraisals of systems. Isaac Newton showed that gravitational pull is a universal force. In so doing, he altered our sense of why an object in space behaves as it does. When Copernicus "removed" the earth from the center of the cosmos, he caused us to change our patterns of thought about the Earth's (and therefore our own) place in the universe.

Cycles and Change

The life cycle of the monarch butterfly illustrates four major changes in the growth and development of that beautiful creature:

egg; larva; pupa; adult. The idea of a cycle is that of an interval of time during which a sequence of a recurring succession or events or phenomena is completed. Thus the life cycle of the monarch has a sense of predictability in terms of time and form. Cycles have not only a theme of recurrence but a circularity about them that makes them different from a pattern of linear development. The classic Greek sense of time and history was cyclical as opposed to the Hebrew sense of time and history which was set more to a vector with beginning, direction, and point and time of destination. Cycles vary greatly in scale so that some are more immediately distinguishable as cycles, as is the cycle of the seasons. Others, like the recurrence of ice ages that appear at least to have some cyclical recurrence are known to us only on the basis of scientific investigation.

In astronomy, a period of time required to bring about the recurrence of certain relative positions (for example, Earth to Sun) or aspects of the heavenly bodies is known as a cycle. The earth orbits the sun every 365+ days, completing a cycle that takes it through its four seasons. In literature, a group of prose or poetic narratives, usually of different authorship, centering on a legendary hero and his associates, is known as a cycle. Thus there is the Arthurian cycle chronicling the noble deeds of King Arthur and his Knights of the Round Table. The Arthurian cycle is often referred to in Medieval romance as the "mater of Britain." The term cyclic poems was first used in late classical times to refer to the independent poems that appeared after Homer to supplement his account of the Trojan War and the homecomings of the heroes.

In music, any compositional form characterized by the repetition, in a later movement or part of the piece, of motives, themes, or whole sections from an earlier movement in order to unify the structure is called a cycle. The need for cyclical devices became ever greater during the times of Mozart and Haydn when the romantic novel took the place of classical drama and narrative poems as the basic model for instrumental music. Thus the idea of the cycle in music took on somewhat new meaning as changes in forms of expression happened in literature and other arts. Thus we see the relationship between cycles and change.

Journeys
Journal
Entry

"The Native Americans who lived here could determine seasons by looking at the stars. One of the easiest ones to recognize as a winter contellation is Orion in the eastern night sky. The Osage believed that they had came from the stars of Orion's belt which they called the Three Deer. Near this formation astronomers have found the famous Great Nebula which has the mass of 10,000 suns! Maybe we all did come from here long ago."

*David Peterson,
7th grade*

WM. BRADFORD

"They made way for the coming of their great sachem, called Massasoit, who came about four or five days later with Squanto, a native of this place. After friendly entertainment and some gifts were given, they made a peace which has now continued...."

William Bradford, 1620

Historians search the events of the past in an attempt to identify cyclical patterns, often with little result. The American historian Arthur Schlesinger, Jr. recently wrote a book in which his thesis was that American political leadership in the twentieth century proceeds in cyclic form from conservative to liberal and back again. These cycles, according to Schlesinger, provide society with a kind of equilibrium.

Economists document cycles of prosperity and hard times in our financial/industrial/commercial system. They point to panics, depressions, and recessions, followed by booms, expansion, and good times. Nations try more or less, depending on the form of government, to intervene with programs during difficult economic times in order to control the cycles artificially. But no one seems to know for sure what causes these cycles even though the effects are evident to the most casual observer.

The rates of change and therefore the recurring patterns of certain cycles vary greatly. Weather changes often within minutes from fair to foul. A person's mood may change abruptly on the basis of some new information. A rousing speech or sermon can change people's opinions in the space of an hour, although the long-term effects may be different. A child watching a pot on the stove wonders if the water will ever boil. Iron rusts quickly in a rainforest environment but slowly in desert conditions. People change as they grow, developing quickly in childhood, more slowly in adulthood, and as they ultimately decline in old age.

The map changes when an empire such as the Soviet Union collapses. The changed map with its new and unfamiliar borders confuses us as we try to learn different place names. But the changed map is merely symbolic of the change-upon-change brought about so rapidly when a seemingly invincible empire dissolves, not on the basis of outside attack, but seemingly from decay within.

The futurist Alvin Toffler has called too much change in too short a time "future shock." Anyone who contemplates buying a personal computer understands the rapidity with which change occurs on the frontiers of technology. A great fear felt by ordinary people is that whatever computer they buy, it will no doubt be obsolete by the time they get it set up at home. Merchandisers play to these fears by exhorting potential customers not to be left behind in the wake of new "breakthroughs." Perhaps one of the best lessons for young learners is to study change and to learn to think about it responsibly and rationally.

One of the obvious conclusions one derives from the Journeys of Discovery curriculum is how exploration and investigation change the world. The Lewis & Clark expedition changed the notion of the United States in terms of its size, its grasp of a continent, its very place in the world as an ocean-to-ocean country in the making. Within a scant fifty years of their epic trek, the United States sent a seagoing expedition to Japan, a foreshadowing of our notion of ourselves as a global presence, and the beginning of an extended and tenuous relationship with that great nation. The travels of Captain James Cook in the late eighteenth century set in place not only the vast holdings of the British Empire but a secure niche for science in the realms of exploration; a major purpose of one of his voyages was to document the transit of Venus. The travels of Marco Polo in the late Middle Ages, on the cusp of the Renaissance, brought about a sense of Eurasia as opposed to a separate Europe and Asia.

Some things change slowly, almost glacially, such as the weathering away of the earth's surface resulting in bizarre rock formations. Some changes appear to be isolated and not susceptible to repetition, and others appear to be perhaps cyclical as the warming and cooling of the earth's atmosphere seem to suggest. Some changes are peaceful, tranquil, such as gently falling snow on green grass, the maturing of a rosebud, or the rising of the moon on a summer night; other changes, such as earthquakes, tornadoes, and volcanic eruptions showcase nature's violent side.

Symmetry and Scale

Human beings are bilateral, that is, one side of our body is nearly a mirror image of the other if one were to draw an axis from the top of our head to the place between our two feet. A

WM. BRADFORD

hen's egg is bilaterally symmetrical if an axis were drawn on it longitudinally, but not if it were drawn around the middle of the egg as if the line were an equator. A circle, no matter where we draw a line from one side to the other through the center, is bi-radially symmetrical. Forms of symmetry, more or less, are found everywhere in nature and in the constructed environment. One finds forms of symmetry in a daffodil, in the Parthenon, in a chambered nautilus, in Dostoevsky's *Crime and Punishment*, in the yin and yang of Eastern philosophy, and in Bach's Brandenburg concerti.

We find symmetry in the seasons, in day and night, and in the configuration of the solar system. Symmetry is found in the leaves of a tree, in the three branches of our government, in the design of the Space Shuttle, in the balance a teacher brings to the curriculum, in our need for both work and play, and in the graceful contours of a Grecian urn.

The converse of symmetry, asymmetry, also exists in our world. The external symmetry of the human is not necessarily found in the placement of our internal organs. No such symmetry can be found in the placement of heart, liver, appendix, etc., although one does find symmetry in the placement of lungs and kidneys. Certain animals, notably sponges and amoeboid protozoans, are asymmetrical in their design. Their shapes are irregular, different for

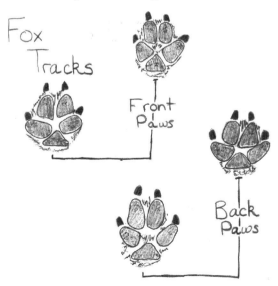

Fox Tracks

Front Paws

Back Paws

each individual, or constantly changing. In the constructed environment, asymmetry is often sought by the constructor, either for aesthetic purposes or because it suits a certain function.

Scale, in cartography, is represented by the ratio between distances on a map and distances on the earth's surface. A scale drawing showing the floor plan of a classroom is an attempt to illustrate the relative size and instances of objects, etc. from each other as they exist in the actual classroom. The more closely the size of features on a map or sketch approaches actual size, the larger is the scale. Thus a map showing the whole earth is considered small-scale, while a map showing a backyard would probably be considered large-scale.

In music, scale is any series of tones arranged in rising or falling order of pitch, or vibrations (cycles) per second. The fewer the vibrations per second, the lower the note, and the more vibrations per second, the higher the note. On a familiar instrument such as the piano, the white keys represent the diatonic scale of seven notes, five of which are whole tones and two of which are half tones. The cycle begins anew with each succeeding octave. This repeating seven note scale can be assembled by a composer in a seemingly infinite variety of combinations to make the many tunes, melodies, etc., which have been written over the years. Of course, the black keys, or sharp notes, each of which is a half-step

"Even today people still use coal to cook and keep warm. Coal is a black or brown rock that can burn for a long period of time which makes it unique. The quality of coal depends on its color and hardness. Anthracite is black and hard while bituminous is softer but also used for these purposes."

Becca Johnson, 6th grade

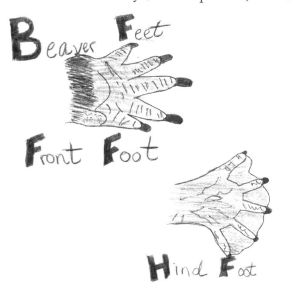

Fox Tracks and Beaver Feet, Ellen Miller, 6th grade

"All the month of May, there was such a quantity of a great sort of flies like for bigness to wasps or bumblebees, which came out of holes in the ground..., and ate the green things, and made such a constant yelling noise as made all the woods ring of them."

William Bradford, 1633

between two given white keys, add to the possibility for variety. Other scales are also possible as shown in Hindu and Arabian music.

Athletic fields and gymnasiums are built to certain scales and symmetries. A football field must be built to an exact size, as must a tennis court; but a baseball field or a basketball court can vary in size. A basketball court must be a true rectangle even though it may be somewhat different in size from one court to another. A baseball field, on the other hand, must be regular only in its infield proportions, that is, from one base to another. The outfield may be allowed to vary so that distances from home plate to the right, center, and left field walls are quite different within a given park as well as from park to park. Thus a baseball field has qualities of symmetry as well as asymmetry.

Interaction and Relationships

Mathmaticians have calculated that the possible number of person-to-person interactions in a room of just ten people reaches into the hundreds. Just imagine a room with thirty or more students. Of course, we interact not only with people but also with nature, the built environment, and so on. Our relationships with others are very different in a classroom where every student works alone at his or her desk versus a room where group projects and cooperative learning are emphasized.

School subjects can themselves be related and allowed to interact or they can be isolated, unrelated, and unconnected. Whether or not there is interaction among people or school subjects in the teaching/learning equation is a fundamental pedagogical question. Where school life is dominated by what the German philosopher Jurgen Habermas calls technical interests, then predictability and control become paramount pedagogical concerns. The technical interest focuses primarily on means-ends questions. An example of this is the use of behavioral objectives. Another example is that of the tightly scripted lesson plan. In other words, any attempt to predict and therefore control the behavior of students toward a predetermined outcome is indicative of the technical interest at work. The result of such a preoccupation is a socially, morally, and intellectually simplified syntax of classroom life.

Habermas identifies another interest, one that he calls the practical interest. The practical interest at work in school life calls for students and teachers to search for understanding about what is being learned. The practical interest encourages relationships and relational learning. It calls for conversation, for working and getting along together, for a sense of integration of people and their experiences. The practical interest is at work when students and teachers engage in project learning, in shared activities, in the constructivist enterprise. The constructivist principle, that experience precedes analysis, is basic to the practical interest.

Habermas identifies a third interest, one that calls on our powers of reflection and insight. Here the questions for a thoughtful consideration of school life takes us to deeper levels. These reflective issues are developed in the Journeys of Discovery curriculum through the recurring questions of utility (Is this useful?), aesthetics (Is this beautiful?), truth (Is this meaningful?), and morality (Is this right?). When those who join the teaching and learning enterprise begin and carry out a process of reflection around these key questions, a different sense of curriculum emerges. This is an empowering curriculum.

Time and Space

History, science, and literature give us insights to time. Geography, art, and geometry illustrate space. Studied together, these disciplines bring time and space together as powerful themes for orienting oneself to one's place in the world. To an adolescent, a year seems a long time. Adults often think in terms of projects for several years. Time and space were one thing to Lewis and Clark when in 1803 they set out for the West Coast of North America. Today someone flies from New York to San Francisco in a matter of hours. Although these modern conveniences such as jet planes, telephones, fax machines, and the Internet are wonderful devices,

WM. BRADFORD

"This spring those Indians who lived about the trading house fell sick of the smallpox and died most miserably; for a sorer disease cannot befall.... The chief sachem himself now died and almost all his friends and kindred."

William Bradford, 1634

they tend to distort our sense of time and space. In this limited sense, the people of the past had a different understanding of these concepts than we do.

In modern life things take on a sense of immediacy. A friend once told of his "nightmare" experience on an overseas trip of being cooped up in a plane with no food served on a runway for six hours, taken off the plane, bused into the city and put into a hotel for two hours of sleep and then taken back to the airport for take-off at 3:00 in the morning only to wait until ater 9:00 a.m., again with no meal served, to take off. Sounds awful, doesn't it? Relative to most airplane flights, it really was a tough experience. Mainly, however, it was an inconvenience. He still made it from Tokyo to Seattle in a time frame measured in hours, not months or weeks. Just imagine the "inconveniences" which Marco Polo, Herodotus, James Cook, and other discoverers of the past experienced.

Today's students are on the receiving end of these distortions of the realities of time and space. Somehow the curricular experience must transcend these limitations in our worldview. This is not a plea to return to those thrilling days of yesteryear. We live in this day and age, and that is our reality. The fact is, however, that most students today have little knowledge of the backdrop of their own existence. In other words, they apparently know little of history,

White Tailed Deer, colored pencil, Justin Taylor, 6th grade

literary portrayals of life in the past, the emergence of artistic and musical forms, etc. Even our own brief national history is a blank slate to many students.

The Journeys of Discovery curriculum represents an attempt among other things to recapture a sense of space and time and place. One of the great experiences of childhood is the sense of wonder. It's easy to forget that simple thought in our rush to "cover" all the things that need to be taught in school. For a student to join in and become a participant on a journey of discovery is far more than an academic study of some epic voyage. It is a union of a young person's desire to learn about his or her world with a participatory engagement in the journey itself.

Time and space are crucial to the musician. Not merely the musical sounds themselves, but the space between the sounds and the timing of the sounds contribute to a symphony. Space is precious to the artist or sculptor. The painter decides how to arrange pigment on the space of a canvas. The sculptor decides how to chip and chisel away space from a block of stone in order to arrive at a finished work. To the mapmaker, lines organize space. Lines form the boundaries, the points of demarcation, etc. that separate or denote one area from another. The beauty of a good map lies not only in its accuracy but also in its elegance as a portrayal of space and place.

"The great epidemic of our day is AIDS and it is creating a major crisis in parts of Africa where vast numbers of children are being raised without parents because both have died from this dreaded disease. For this reason, many are moving to large cities where they live as street kids or in overcrowded orphanages. Something needs to be done to help them...."

Eileen Reilly, 7th grade

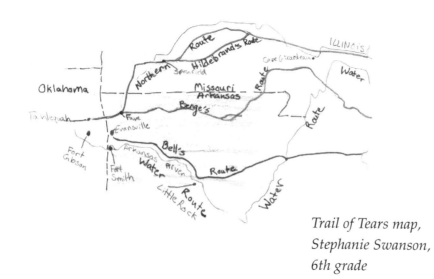

Trail of Tears map, Stephanie Swanson, 6th grade

WM. BRADFORD

Equilibrium and Order

When disequilibrium occurs, for example, in war or in family problems, disorder follows close behind. When feelings, thoughts, and actions are harmonious, equilibrium and order result. Young people desperately need balance (equilibrium) and predictability (order) in their lives. Teachers know this better than anyone. They work daily with students who bring with them equilibrium and order as well as its converse.

The idea of equilibrium applies well to systems theory. Any system, for instance, a traffic system, maintains much of its equilibrium by balancing the rate and flow of traffic with a network of light, signs, patrols, etc. When the system is in a state of equilibrium and good order, traffic flows smoothly. But unfortunate events (a rush hour pile up) can quickly throw the smoothest system out of balance. In the balance of nature disequilibrium can occur in an ecosystem when previously outside elements are introduced. An example of this is the introduction of rabbits to the Australian ecosystem. The system, in its more natural state of balance, was not equipped to accommodate the influx of such widely ranging animals. Many attempts have been made to restore balance to the system, with mainly limited results.

In the Pacific Northwest of the United States, the building of several large dams, Grand Coulee, Bonneville, and others, has made the river system far more orderly and therefore more predictable. For purposes of flood control, hydroelectricity, irrigation, and recreation, the system of dams has been a considerable success. On the other hand, the equilibrium of elements of the system has been thrown into disorder. Two examples of this are the greatly diminished salmon run on the Columbia and the displaced river-dwelling Indian tribes who for centuries had made their livelihood at such sites as Celilo Falls, now submerged beneath the waters of the reservoir created by one of the dams. Other more subtle changes may not be accurately assessed for years to come.

The warming and cooling cycles of the earth's atmosphere have a long-term scale of order and equilibrium not easily determined in the short run. Recent scientific evidence points to a warming effect and a diminishment of the ozone layer. Whether this is part of a long-term change of equilibrium is not known. The Earth, as part of the solar system, is situated at a point of delicate balance in its distance from the sun. This balance is necessary in order to maintain temperature conditions conducive to life forms as we know them. When the quality of the Earth's atmosphere changes because of increased cattle grazing and increased automobile exhaust, the system is altered. The system's ability to restore itself is problematic.

It took human beings thousands of years to discern the order of the seasons and the attendant implications to the point that they could make the change from hunting and gathering to agriculture. Once systems of agriculture were established in place of systems of hunting and gathering, the need for order in agriculture, laws, roads, and the many shared functions of permanently settled people emerged.

Summary

Each of the themes is connected to the others in ways that make the continual revisiting of them all necessary. Thus while content may change from unit to unit and from year to year in the Journeys of Discovery curriculum, the themes remain as conceptual points of reference. The themes have the power of ideas, and ideas are the mortar which holds together the curricular building blocks.

Thematic, interdisciplinary teaching and learning are at the heart of the Journeys of Discovery curriculum. The commitment is to reducing the sheer amount of information that students need to learn in order to be successful while putting a premium on the quality of what they learn. Carefully selected themes housed within a goal structure of broad ideas are the keys to thinking about meaningful curriculum. When the themes are directed toward a goal structure that honors the criteria of utility, social responsibility, the intrinsic value of knowledge, philosophical value, and childhood enrichment, then the first steps to an improved teaching and learning environment will have been taken.

Journeys
Career Profile

"I learned that being a meteorologist would be a fun career because you get to look at maps from space that help form predictions about the coming weather. This is very helpful to pilots, farmers, and people who travel. Important areas of study include science, mathematics, and writing. "

Brian McNeilly, 7th grade

IX

Moral Education

Sidebars:
The Chronicles of Crèvecoeur, Franklin, and Bartram

DE CRÈVECOEUR

Increasingly, there is the demand that the schools "do some thing" about moral education. Widespread agreement exists that teachers and students should address not only the curriculum of subject matter but questions of morality as well. Problems arise, however, when this demand is taken seriously by school personnel because people have difficulty agreeing on exactly what form and content such moral education might take. As the country becomes increasingly pluralistic and multicultural, the issues of moral education become even more complex. Often times there is the suspicion that certain groups, religious or secular, are attempting to foist their views on others. A typical response has been to attempt to avoid the matter as much as possible. The problem with this is that any thoughtful observer can readily see that moral education takes place in school settings, for better or worse, whether we claim it does or not. The teacher who demands punctuality from pupils makes a moral point. The teacher who punishes students for cheating on an exam is teaching morality. The teacher who ignores certain students while granting favors to others is teaching a kind of morality.

So, if one agrees with the point that moral education happens inevitably in any classroom setting, the questions arise whether we can agree that morals and values should be taught *consciously*, *which ones* are most important, and *how* might they be taught. Most people would agree with the assumption that knowledge without morality is a dangerous thing. Mohandas Gandhi himself identified "knowledge without character" as one of humankind's major sins.

The Greek philosopher Socrates wondered whether morality could be taught in the same sense that, say, geometry can be taught. If so, then it should become a school subject and a major part of the curriculum. But Socrates in his wisdom decided that morality cannot be taught in the same manner that geometry can be taught. Of course he was perfectly right. This is so because a school subject such as mathematics or science represents a set of information, ideas, and procedures to be learned, generally for academic purposes, while morality asks more of someone. We would hope that mathematicians and scientists have a moral compass, but morality is itself the internalizing and acting on that moral compass.

The conclusion we have reached regarding moral education in putting together the Journeys of Discovery curriculum is the same one we have reached with regard to the curriculum of history, the arts, science, geography, literature, etc. Our conclusion is that the center of gravity needs to shift from teaching to learning. Notice, for example, that Socrates' question was whether morality could be *taught* successfully. Our question is slightly different. Can morality be *learned*? The answer to that is obvious: of course it can and inevitably is. It happens all the time, primarily through situation, action, and example. And that is precisely how we propose to conduct a program of moral education. Just as we have encouraged teachers to stop trying to "teach" so much geography, mathematics, etc., and to instead create an environment for learning these subjects, so do we propose the same approach to moral education. Journeys of Discovery asks more of students and teachers than that they acquire academic knowledge. This curriculum requires that students and teachers *become* discoverers themselves. In this sense, the discovery process becomes something one internalizes and acts on. Likewise, we can begin by offering students the opportunity to internalize and act on moral precepts such as responsibility, persistance, and respect.

As students read the journals of Lewis & Clark, they encounter the deep and abiding friendship of these explorers, the loyalty they felt toward mission and country, and the hope and the courage these explorers exhibited. Students read of Lewis & Clark's respect for the dignity of others when they consider the vote taken by the entire Corps of Discovery, one which gives us a glimpse of

DE CRÈVECOEUR

"My bees afford me the most pleasing and extensive themes;... their government, their industry, their quarrels, their passions, always present me with something new; for which reason, when weary of labor, my common place of rest is under my locust trees, close by my beehouse."

J. Hector St. John de Crèvecoeur, 1782

the first recorded vote by an African American, York, and the first recorded vote by a Native American and woman, Sacajawea. But such glimpses alone are not enough. They can be read at the level of information, material for test items only. The power comes from allowing students and teachers to reflect on the values and to exhibit them in their own lives through their school work and through community action.

There is an old cliche that states that values are "better caught than taught." Like so many old sayings, it contains much truth. When we look carefully at the saying, something significant emerges, that is, the center of gravity shifts from "taught" (teacher) to "caught" (learner). In other words you can't catch something, whether it's a baseball or an idea, without getting actively involved and taking on some responsibilty. Something else of significance emerges; that is, if values are to be caught, then they must pre-exist. Journeys of Discovery does not encourage students to "invent" their own moral values; rather the emphasis is on discovering the power of time-honored values in the lives of explorers, scientists, artists, etc., and in their own lives. The poet Robert Frost characterized education as "hanging around until you've caught on." The emphasis is Journeys of Discovery on active learning, team building, engagement, and constructivist themes provides students and teachers with a wide range of situations and opportuni-

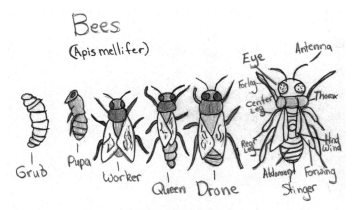

Bee Life Stages,
Mollie Mors,
6th grade

ties to "catch on" to those things that are important in life, to develop uplifting moral logic, choice and action. Thus we come around to the point made by Socrates that the direct teaching of morals and values offers little promise of meaningful outcome. But the power of a curriculum of inspiration, hope, and dignity to offer a matrix in which to consider and act on what is right, what is just, and what is beautiful should not be underestimated.

Having established our view that moral education is necessary in school settings and having described our perspective that moral issues ought to come through the course of study rather than be taught separately, we turn our thoughts to the matter of exactly which values should be emphasized. We propose a list of ten. There is nothing new about these values. They are very traditional. They have stood the test of time. Wise people in many different cultural settings have concluded that they are basic to a well-ordered, purposeful life. In this sense, they represent a distillation of what is best about the human condition. They give us a goal structure.

We have divided our list of moral values into two categories: substantive and procedural. The substantive values include courage, wisdom, justice, respect, and responsibility. The procedural values include persistence, tolerance, organization, curiosity, and collaboration. Substantive values are the more basic. Without

Journeys
Journal
Entry

"Each spring the orchardists in our area depend upon bees for pollination which is necessary to fertilize each blossom so fruit can grow. I looked at some grains of pollen under a microscope and saw the most amazing things! Did you know that...?

*Heidi Lewis,
7th grade*

*Crab Apple Branch, watercolor,
Amanda Thompson,
8th grade*

BEN FRANKLIN

"My father's little library consisted chiefly of books in polemic divinity.... Plutarch's Lives *was there, in which I read abundantly, and I still think that time spent to great advantage. There was also a book of Defoe's, called an* Essay on Projects, *and another of Dr. Mather's, called* Sayings to do Good *which perhaps gave me a turn of thinking that had an influence on some of the principal future events of my life."*

Benjamin Franklin, 1771

them, the procedural values have little to recommend them. This is to say that when the substantive values are internalized, the procedural values take on great merit because they represent how we get things done in life, whether in school, at home, at work, or other settings. These ten values jump off the pages of the Journeys of Discovery curriculum. In that sense they are organic, not pasted on or otherwise artificially contrived. Teachers and students using Journeys of Discovery will find example after example in the lives of the great discoverers. And the nature of the assignments calls for students themselves to act on the very values modeled by the virtuous men and women whose dicoveries they read about.

Additionally, the curriculum itself is based on these ten values. For example, we have constructed the activities and materials in ways that we feel will enhance curiosity, encourage collaboration, and create conditions of discovery. An example of substantive value inclusion in the curriculum can be seen in the respect with which teachers and students are treated. We have long been convinced that students and teachers are intelligent enough to read original source material. Thus the curriculum is based on such subject matter: journals, diaries, ships' logs, maps, artwork, stories, music, and other forms of direct access to knowledge that cuts out the "middlemen" of dumbed-down textbooks and other secondary sources of information.

Classroom Museum Display

Another example of curriculum integration with positive values is found in the reflective thinking sessions that we are convinced are so fundamental to learning. Students are encouraged to seek justice, wisdom, truth, and beauty as they reflect on the activities in which they are engaged. Assessment merges seamlessly with teaching and learning in sessions where students are challenged to decide for themselves not merely *what* they have learned but how valuable, truthful, and useful it may be. And it should be obvious even to the most casual observer that the Journeys of Discovery curriculum emphasizes persistence and responsibility. The life habits, so needed in the family, the neighborhood, the workplace, and school are as much a part of the curriculum as are the skills and knowledge students are expected to acquire.

Conclusion

Journeys of Discovery is an integrated curriculum in the fullest sense. The patterns of integration include bringing students and teachers together in a spirit of caring and collaboration, infusing the subject matter with the best of the arts and sciences in the search for lasting, purposful ideas, inviting students to take responsibility for their own learning with all that that implies, and creating a reflective environment in which students and teachers can search for meaning.

Journeys
Journal
Entry

"My favorite book is by Madeline L'Engle and is titled A Wrinkle in Time. *It tells the story of a girl about my age named Meg who has a most amazing younger brother. Together they meet a funny old woman who actually turns out to be an angel and takes them to a most unusual world to save their father from a terrible evil...."*

Bonnie Lewis,
7th grade

Standards and Assessment

Sidebars:
The Expeditions of Lewis & Clark and Zebulon Pike

Lewis & Clark

It is tempting to view the standards movement as a time to go "back to the basics," to "get tough" with students while raising teacher performance at the same time. For some this means a retreat from projects, integrated studies, and collaborative approaches to more narrowly focused single-subject, skills-based teaching. A teacher recently said that she no longer does project learning with her students because of the pressures she feels from the state tests given at year's end to determine to what extent her students have achieved the standards. There are many such stories. Typically they are based on a belief that the royal road to higher scores is paved with the good intentions of old-fashioned textbook-driven drill and practice seat-work. There is, however, little evidence that this approach will work, and little support for it in the reports of professional associations and education research studies.

State and National Standards

In recent years the various professional associations have weighed in with content standards for their respective disciplines. These groups include the National Council for Teachers of Mathematics (NCTM), the International Reading Association (IRA), the National Council of Teachers of English (NCTE), the National Council for the Social Studies (NCSS), the National Science Teachers Association (NSTA), and others. In each case, the attempt has been to clarify the essence of the various school subjects and to reach agreement on what constitutes essential learning. This seems eminently reasonable, useful, and enabling to teachers and students alike. Appropriate content is better defined by setting benchmarks. Appropriate assessment procedures should be used to determine the extent to which students are achieving the benchmarks.

The biggest problem associated with the standards movement is the misinterpretation of their intent. Their purpose was never to force teachers and students back to a narrow perimeter of textbooks and worksheets. Rather, their intent was to provide common agreement as to what constitutes appropriate learning in the various disciplines and to close gaps found along the way from goals to experiences to assessment.

Let us examine a distillation of the recommendations for how teachers and students might best achieve in light of the standards established by the professional associations. These recommendations come not from one or two of the associations but from all of them. They may come as a surprise to those who would contend that the best way to achieve the standards is to go "back to the basics."

Zemelman, Daniels, and Hyde, in their insightful book, *Best Practice: New Standards for Teaching and Learning in America's Schools*, identify common recommendations which flow from the national curriculum reports of the various professional associations. They sort the recommendations into the two categories of "more emphasis" and "less emphasis." Moreover, agreement on the principles is so compelling that it constitutes an "unrecognized consensus."

National Recommendations and Key Principles

- LESS whole-class, teacher-directed instruction, e.g., lecturing
- LESS student passivity: sitting, listening, receiving, and absorbing information
- LESS classroom time devoted to fill-in-the-blank worksheets, dittos, workbooks, and other "seatwork"
- LESS student time spent reading textbooks and basal readers
- LESS attempt by teachers to thinly "cover" large amounts of material in every subject area
- MORE experiential, inductive, hands-on learning

"The president who sent Lewis and Clark on their expedition was Thomas Jefferson. He was a remarkable man who designed his own home, Monticello, which means 'Little Mountain.' He worked on this special place for thirty years and it was surrounded by 5,000 acres of rolling hills of cropland and forest. He once said, 'I am as happy nowhere else, and all my wishes end where I hope my days end, at Monticello.'"

*Angie Denallo,
6th grade*

- MORE active learning in the classroom, with all the attendant noise and movement of students doing, talking, and collaborating
- MORE emphasis on higher-order thinking; learning a field's key concepts and principles
- MORE deep study of a smaller number of topics, so students internalize the field's way of inquiry
- MORE time devoted to reading whole, original, real books and nonfiction materials
- MORE choice for students; e.g., picking their own books, writing topics, team partners, research projects

Zemelman, Daniels, and Hyde also identify the following "interlocking principles, assumptions, or theories" that they note as fundamental to the "more" and "less" recommendations.

STUDENT-CENTERED. The best starting point for schooling is kids' real interests; all across the curriculum, investigating students' own questions should always take precedence over studying arbitrarily and distantly selected "content."

EXPERIENTIAL. Active, hands-on, concrete experience is the most powerful and natural form of learning. Students should be immersed in the most direct possible experience of the content of every subject.

REFLECTIVE. Balancing the immersion in direct experience must be opportunities for learners to look back, to reflect, to debrief, to abstract from their experiences what they have felt, thought, and learned.

AUTHENTIC. Real, rich, complex ideas and materials are at the heart of the curriculum. Lessons or textbooks which water down, control, or over-simplify content ultimately disempower students.

HOLISTIC. Students learn best when they encounter whole, real ideas, events, and materials in purposeful contexts, and not by studying sub-parts isolated from actual use.

DEMOCRATIC. The classroom is a model community; students learn what they live as citizens of the school.

CONSTRUCTIVIST. Students do not just receive content; in a very real sense, they recreate and re-invent every cognitive system they encounter, including language, literacy, and mathematics.

Our attempt in their brief overview to the standards movement has been to illustrate the futility in attempting to achieve the spirit, even the letter, of the standards by retreating to instruction characterized by seat-work, worksheets, isolated students and subjects, and rote learning of skills basically out of any meaningful context. The evidence, if one accepts the recommendations of the professional educational associations, is quite to the contrary.

The argument for experiential, highly-engaged, collaborative, reflective, democratic classrooms is, in fact, an argument for integrated studies and interdisciplinary approaches to the curriculum. This is what such approaches do best. They challenge students and teachers to work together to solve meaningful problems, to carry out projects too complex and involved for people to always do alone, and to create the conditions where connections are natural and made among enduring ideas and values.

Learning Assessment

The old paradigm was one of assessment as a "outside event." That is to say that both teachers and students tended to view tests, quizzes, and other forms of evaluation as disconnected from learning experiences. The idea was that a test was a kind of "time out" designed to find out what students know. An unfortunate outcome of this perception was the common problem that what was tested often bore scant congruence to what was taught and supposedly learned. The only difference between quizzes and teacher-made tests on the one hand and standardized tests on the other was one of scale.

Gradually a new paradigm has emerged in which standards are being set for what constitutes essential learnings, and assessment is being integrated into teaching and learning experiences in more naturalistic ways. The result is a more tightly coupled

Journeys Journal Entry

"What I liked most about the story of Lewis and Clark is how they never gave up trying to accomplish their mission. If it wasn't for them we might not be living in this nice part of America today. They were very brave to go to places strange to them and make so many new friends. Most of all, they were friends and always helped each other out...."

Hector Gonzales, 7th grade

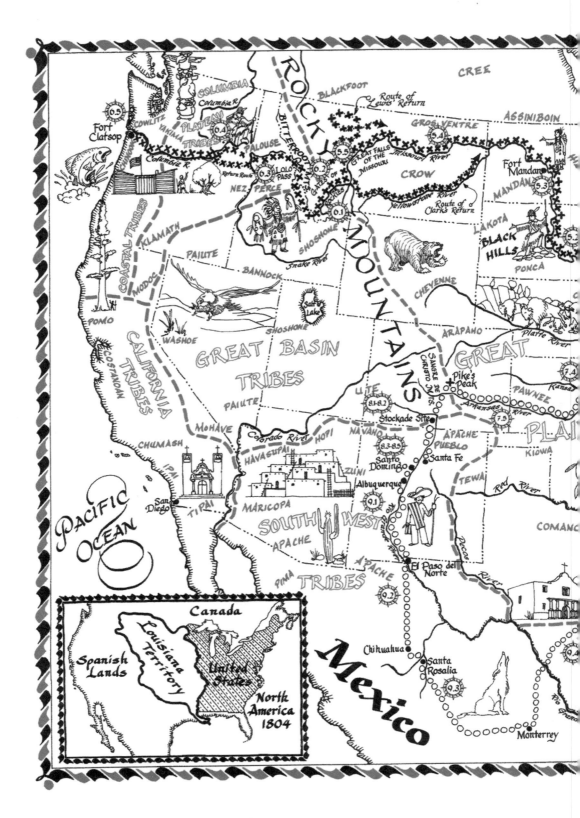

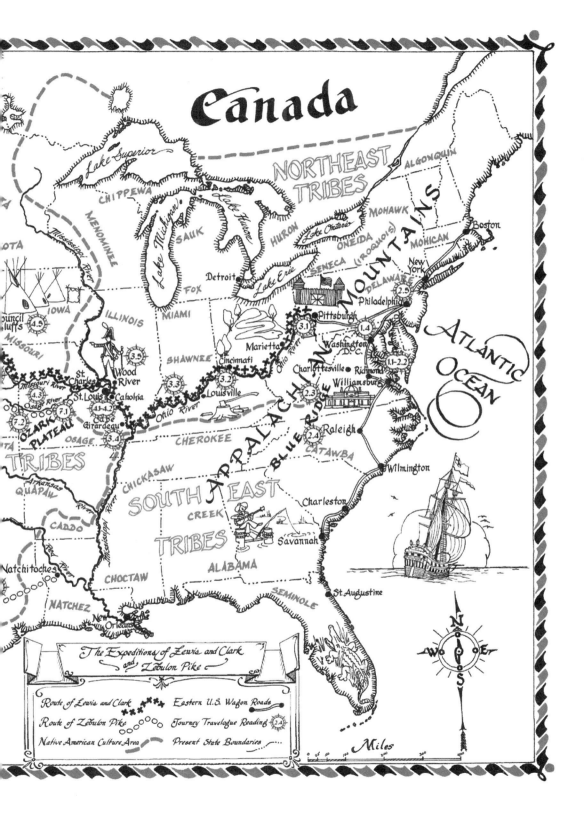

Canada

Lake Superior

CHIPPEWA

NORTHEAST TRIBES

ALGONQUIN

MENOMINEE

Lake Michigan

Lake Huron

MOHAWK

Lake Ontario

HURON

ONEIDA

MOHICAN

Boston

SAUK

Lake Erie

SENECA (IROQUOIS)

New York

FOX

Detroit

DELAWARE

2.5

Philadelphia

Mississippi River

IOWA

ILLINOIS

MIAMI

3.1

Pittsburgh

1.4

Council Bluffs

4.5

Marietta

Washington D.C.

MISSOURI

3.5

SHAWNEE

Cincinnati

Ohio River

Charlottesville

Richmond

1.1–2.2

ATLANTIC OCEAN

St. Charles

Wood River

3.3

3.2

Williamsburg

Missouri River

4.3

St. Louis

Cahokia

Louisville

2.3

4.1–4.2

APPALACHIAN MOUNTAINS

7.2

Osage River

7.1

Cape Girardeau

3.4

2.4

Raleigh

OZARK PLATEAU

OSAGE

CHEROKEE

BLUE RIDGE

CATAWBA

TRIBES

Wilmington

Arkansas River

QUAPAW

CHICKASAW

SOUTHEAST

CADDO

CREEK

Charleston

Red River

Mississippi River

TRIBES

Savannah

Natchitoches

CHOCTAW

ALABAMA

NATCHEZ

SEMINOLE

St. Augustine

New Orleans

N
W E
S

The Expeditions of Lewis and Clark
and Zebulon Pike

Route of Lewis and Clark   Eastern U.S. Wagon Roads
Route of Zebulon Pike   Journey Travelogue Reading   2.4
Native American Culture Area   Present State Boundaries

Miles

LEWIS & CLARK

"The doctor presented me with two handsome specimens, the one a grinder of the elephant, the other, that of a mammoth, the former weighs ten and one-half pounds, the latter I have not weighed, from the circumstance of its roots being attached to a lump of clay."

Meriwether Lewis, 1803

curriculum in which standards, classroom teaching, and assessment are merged into a coherent whole. As assessment is integrated into the normal routines of classroom life, it begins to inform students and teachers of progress in learning along the way, which is far different from the old perception of test as outside event.

Thus even the essential purpose of assessment changes from one of an emphasis on sorting students out from high to low enabling each student to know how to improve. To be sure, there will always be tests, teacher-made and standardized, that sort students into academic categories, but that is not our focus here beyond saying that the effective use of the newer assessment techniques will in fact improve student scores on formal tests.

Integrated studies and interdisciplinary curricula lend themselves quite readily to the new paradigm. When students are encouraged to learn from primary source materials, when they are encouraged to think of learning as problem-solving and inquiry, and when they plan, work, and reflect together, assessment becomes an integral part of the enterprise. Real problems demand real assessment, and projects can be displayed and subjected to performance-assessment criteria in much the same way the drama, music, and athletics performances are. Because integrated studies seek connections rather than separation and isolation, so too do the means of assessing learning.

Our emphasis here is on assessment that is integrated, ongoing, and authentic. Teachers and students should consider that the best way to learn is to practice continuous reflection on learning. Assessment is far more than test results. Assessment at its best asks the questions we have posed elsewhere in Journeys of Discovery. The questions are simple, but they go to the heart of the matter: "Is this meaningful?" "Is this truthful?" "Is this beautiful?" "Is this helpful?" This is the essence of assessment in integrated studies. To place the emphasis elsewhere, for example, merely in test-measured achievement items, is to completely miss the truth of assessment and its potential to inform, to improve, to reach for the best in learning.

Integrated studies will not work particularly well unless teachers and students are first integrated. But integration implies more than integrating people and even subject matter. It implies integrating everything, and that must include assessment. It is an old adage but an insightful one that if you want to bring about fundamental improvement in a situation, then everything must change.

What are the implications for such a daring move? Will test scores plummet? Will achievement diminish? We are convinced that such unfavorable outcomes will not transpire because of both qualitative and quantitative evidence indicating achievement gains made by students who experience interdisciplinary studies. But even those who basically agree that assessment must be integrated along with everything else will often tell us they simply do not know how to do it. For this reason twenty activities are suggested that can be integrated with everyday learning experiences in classrooms regardless of the subject matter under consideration. We urge you to try them faithfully, and as you do, to assess your own sense of how everything changes.

What changes should you expect? First, you will not be able to "cover" as much material. This is all to the good since the recommendations coming from the professional associations all tend to agree that selected, in-depth coverage is better anyway. Secondly, you will find that the amount of conversation increases in the classroom. Again, this is a promising change because the evidence from learning research is clear that when students talk about what they are doing, what they are learning, comprehension increases along with vocabulary and related thought processes. And thirdly, achievement will increase. Why? Because you will have created a metacognitive environment in which students and teachers reflect thoughtfully on what they are doing, which takes us back to the four questions posed earlier.

A brief summary follows of several learning strategies designed to integrate assessment with the routines of classroom life. As you implement these strategies, and as they become an integral part of teaching and learning in your classroom, you will experience a fundamental change toward a reflective, thoughtful, and

Journeys
Journal
Entry

"We grabbed a few provisions and returned to the time machine. Raymond put the skin sample into a little slot and typed the word prehistoric elephant *on the keyboard. Within two minutes the door opened and it appeared that we were standing somewhere in a dry grassland. Grazing in the distance as a moeritherium...."*

Sydney Gossard,
6th grade

Lewis & Clark

"There was a large mound in the midst of the (Nebraska) plain.... The Indians have made it a great article to their superstition. It is called the Mountain of Little People, or Little Spirit, and they believe it is the abode of little devils in human form, about 18 inches high and with remarkably large heads. They are armed with sharp arrows with which they are very skillful."

Meriwether Lewis, 1804

caring learning community.

Integrated Learning Strategies

I LEARNED STATEMENTS. The "I Learned" statement is a simple but effective means of allowing every student to reflect on a lesson at its close. Here is how it works. When you have basically finished a lesson or activity, ask each student to write on a piece of paper something significant he or she learned. This is an open-ended device, not a fishing expedition for the "right" answer. Typically, you should allow no more than five minutes for students to write down their thoughts. By the way, it is a good idea for the teacher to write and "I Learned" statement as well. Don't expect too much the first time you attempt this with your class. Some students will have difficulty thinking of anything to write. This is so because they never may have been asked this question before, perhaps they have never been asked to reflect. In time, they will get better at it. Use some of the more insightful examples of student writing to prime the pump. Read them out loud so that those who are having trouble will begin to get the idea. Keep in mind that the collection of 'I Learned' statements you just gathered from your class represents probably the single best sense of what was learned.

THINK ALOUD. It has been shown that average and slower

Early American Legends Puppet Theatre

learners are especially disadvantaged when they are given little or no opportunity to process ideas as they attmept to take them in. The "Think Aloud" strategy is designed to allow learners to move their own interior and often faulty logic into a "market place." Here is how it works. At some point in an activity, perhaps following some explanation by the teacher, students are asked to work together in pairs to discuss what they are learning, and how well they understand it, to give examples, etc. This ususally takes about five to ten minutes. When students discuss their ideas, misconceptions as well as understandings are placed out in the open. This reflective activity allows peer teaching or coaching, and it provides a reasonably private forum for checking for understanding.

I CAN TEACH. Aristotle wrote some twenty-five centuries ago that one of the best ways to learn something is to teach it. Taking a cue from the great philosopher, ask your students to teach the skill, knowledge, idea, etc. they learned in a particular lesson or activity. This can be done as a homework assignment in which students teach their parents, siblings, or someone else. Having students teach important things they are learning gives them a chance to revisit the material from another perspective (that of teacher), and it serves as a good awareness link to the home. Another variation is to have middle school students teach younger

Younger Guest-Critics

"The legend told by Mrs. Schuster that I liked best was about Coyote's race between the two rivers. It reminded me of the Tortise and Hare tale because it teaches that it is better to go slow and do things right than rush through them."

Jeanette Thompson, 7th grade

Lewis & Clark

"Glad of an opportunity of being able to converse more intelligibly, Sakakawea came into a tent with the captains, sat down and was beginning to interpret when, in the person of Cameahwait, she recognized her brother. She instantly jumped up and ran and embraced him throwing over him her blanket and weeping profusely."

Meriwether Lewis, 1805

children. This gives them an opportunity to think through and act on how they could simplify the procedures in order for young children to understand an idea.

Of course, there are other ways to create a reflective assessment environment, but we think that if you begin with these three simple techniques you will begin to see how it works. (For more ideas and additional theory behind reflective assessment with middle school students, see Arthur K. Ellis, *Teaching, Learning, and Assessment Together: The Reflective Classroom* [Eye on Education, Inc., 2001]).

George Shannon, teenage member of Lewis & Clark's Expedition, colored pencil, Ellen Miller, 6th grade

Technology and
Community

Sidebars:
The Adventures of John & Jessie Fremont and Kit Carson

the FREMONTS

"I collected in the neighborhood of St. Louis twenty-one men, principally Creole and Canadian voyageurs, who had become familiar with prairie life in the service of the fur companies in the Indian country. [Kit] Carson was our guide."

John Fremont, 1842

For Alfred the Great, champion of feudal England and medieval learning, life was a quest "to know all that I have long wished to understand." Eleanor of Aquitaine's passion for knowing and adventure was legendary. The ballads and chronicles of her contemporaries praise the queen's "nobility of mind" as well as being "indefatigable for every undertaking." Marco Polo sought to experience "the world and its wonders" and Thomas Jefferson issued the redoubtable challenge for Lewis & Clark to "learn all you can." What manner of person states a raison d'etre in such boundless terms? Those who aspire to the spirit of discovery and exploration realize the significance of understanding broadly expressed. To be human is to seek a fuller awareness of ourselves and our world by looking inward and outward, to the past and future, so we can attach meaning to present experience and improve our lives in both intellectual and practical terms.

Great exemplars of lifelong learning gained knowledge and insight for the pure joy of understanding as well as for the pragmatic aspects of building success in human affairs. Expansive learning is James Cook pondering the fate of South Pacific Islanders whose world would be forever changed by those who would follow in his wake. It is also his ingenuity in saving the *Endeavor* after the Great Barrier Reef tore into its hull thousands of miles from safe harbor. Expansive learning is Eleanor Roosevelt striving to bring East Bloc nations to the negotiating table for the U.N. Declaration on Human Rights while working to place safeguards on America's peaceful use of atomic energy.

Facilitating each generation's contribution to expansive learning were breakthroughs in science and technology. Contemporaries of Herodotus in Greece's Golden Age, Hippocrates of Cos uncovered relationships between environment and disease to open new realms of medical treatment, while Appolonius of Perga devised the mathematical principles upon which the astrolabe was built. That instrument together with the compass, possibly a Chinese invention, would guide Columbus and a host of other mariners across unknown seas in the fifteenth century. Technological innovation today is unfolding at an unprecedented rate in ways that are creating a new paradigm for education. The new technologies for learning enable anyone to more fully engage in the captivating and timeless enterprise of expansive learning.

Multidimensional Pathways for Expansive Learning

Four basic aspects of exploration characterize its successful undertaking in any age: direction, means, community, and most importantly, mission. Direction in times past implied one's linear course overland, at sea, or through space under the limitations of time and place. Marco Polo's father and uncle directed a course to the Far East across the Great Silk Road. European cartographers in the next century incorporated newly acquired knowledge regarding the Orient onto their maps with that region so positioned to give rise to the term "orienteering." But exploration today through interactive learning technologies no longer confines the student-explorer to the limitations of linear time and space. Like travel itineraries, books and articles have been organized into beginnings, middles, and ends. The new orientation, however, is multidimensional and offers video programming, text resources, and other media providing powerful means through which learners can stop to investigate, return to a point of interest, fast forward, or move to an entirely new course quite at will. Certain knowledge and considerable skill development is fostered through progressive instruction, but this should not diminish the power that multidimensional learning brings to the educational environment.

Journeys
Journal
Entry

"We started our journey on Thursday, September 21st at 8:54 a.m. and headed west. The leaves on the trees were changing colors and beginning to fall. We wanted to learn about the three vegetation zones of our area, desert shrub, prairie grassland, and forest. The data I gathered showed some interesting information...."

Emily Boone, 7th grade

The FREMONTS

"This morning we caught the first faint glimpse of the Rocky Mountains, about sixty miles distant. About eight, we discerned several persons on horseback a mile or two ahead. We found them to be two white men, and a black named Jim Beckwourth, who had left St. Louis as a boy to live with the Crow Indians."

John Fremont, 1842

Technological Means for Interaction

The means of exploration has ranged from walking and eyesight to sea voyaging and Hubble Telescope viewing. Each method has contributed to important steps forward in the human adventure to understand ourselves and the world around us. Each remains vital to renewing our shared world. Just as the appearance of the North Atlantic stern-rudder and the Mediterranean lanteen rig joined forces to launch Europe's Age of Discovery, so new technologies for instruction can propel students into dynamic new realms of learning. Web-based classrooms enable students to become curriculum developers themselves by opening doors to a vast knowledge base in digital form with access to the Library of Congress, Smithsonian Institution, National Geographic Society, and a multitude of other educational organizations with sites specifically devoted to the interests of young people.

Expansive learning enables students to construct and assemble new understanding themselves rather than depend solely on the teacher for dispensing knowledge. The approach is liberating to educators who find themselves assuming more the role of facilitator in coursework associated with research and reporting. But these methods hold special significance for students since, as Seymour Papert has observed, "The scandal of education is that every time you teach something, you deprive a child of the pleasure and ben-

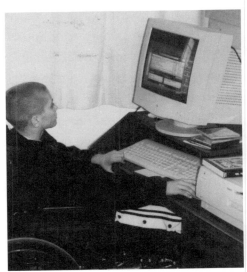

www.nationalgeographic.com

efit of discovery." The Teaching with Technology initiative in Idaho links students in schools throughout the state who share information they have gathered in science class through software probes to conduct water quality studies in accordance with the scientific method. Virtual field trips are arranged for social studies instruction to the National Environmental and Engineering Laboratory to acquaint students with federal efforts to improve water quality on public lands. Language arts teachers have established their own websites to showcase student writing and compare assessment techniques using a six-trait quality writing rubric. Profiles of student work are maintained in electronic files to create a comprehensive portfolio of coursework throughout the year. The portfolio becomes an important component for the reporting of student progress and to formulate academic improvement plans.

Web-based Community Building

Of central importance to successful exploration is the formation of community. The great achievements that renew societies' greatness are not won as solitary endeavors. Rather, a team is formed to complete a mission and participants are often drawn from diverse backgrounds as contrasting perspectives invariably invigorate the group efforts. Lewis & Clark's Corps of Discovery

"Our criteria for Journeys study guide website selections are that they are both educational and appealing to students. By exploring a homepage, other doors to various realms of knowledge are reached simply by clicking on different links. This broadens our knowledge and shows how everything in the world is connected in some way—an idea that is central to the Journeys curriculum."

Nick Siler

"Pioneers would pack their household items in the grain they brought from wherever they came from to plant where they were going to settle. Along the way they would stop to cook and eat. In using their dishes and cookware, small weed seeds that had been mixed up in the grain would be deposited and sometimes take over native species. This is still happening today with invaders like the yellow star thistle that is so hard to control around here."

*Derek Miller,
7th grade*

KIT CARSON

"The smallpox broke out among the [Ute] Indians while they were on their way to their hunting grounds.... They came to the conclusion that the Superintendent [of Indian Affairs] was the cause of this affliction. He had given a blanket coat to each of the headmen, ...and the Indians firmly believed that the coats were the cause of their deaths."

*Kit Carson,
1854*

exemplifies the advantages of such arrangements. Drawn together for common cause were thirty adults, two teenagers, and a baby. Most of the men were assigned to the expedition from the army but the interpreters and hunters were civilians, as were Sakakawea and York. The two captains allowed both of them, incidently, to vote on important decisions in a day when this right was not accorded to women and blacks.

An enhanced sense of community inclusiveness is similarly fostered through the deployment of new learning technologies. Just as successful exploration demanded cooperation, so the more demanding tasks of expansive learning through collective research, problem-solving, and reporting invite teamwork. Moreover, the learning community is no longer limited to instructional settings at school or in the home. Communities are defined in terms of an affiliation with a shared identity. This identity may be rooted in values or interests but it invariably requires the exchange of ideas and sense of familiarity that grows in strength over time because the identity is reinforced through routines, stories, and meaningful experiences. The development of social structure defined in such terms is of critical importance to individual wellbeing at any age, and especially for young people who often associate self-worth with affiliation. The digital world is well suited to afford young people the ability to form communities to develop new understandings and positive relationships. To be sure, threats exist in the form of online exploiters which is why supervision is as essential in digital communities as in those of the real world.

Critics of interactive learning environments might benefit from the example of Sir Joseph Banks. Banks's credentials distinguished him as one of Europe's most prominent naturalists of the nineteenth century and the longest serving president of Britain's Royal Society. He intended to participate as chief scientist on James Cook's epic second Pacific voyage. But when Banks learned that specifications Cook deemed essential for *Resolution's* seaworthiness did not afford him circumstances to which he was accustomed, the scientist promptly resigned. This decision prevented his participation in what has been termed the greatest voyage from the time of Magellan's circumnavigation to the flight of Apollo XI. Limitations in the deployment of instructional technology certainly exist today but should not preclude its proper use. One valuable purpose is to extend community building in the digital world generating new friendships and understandings among students and teachers throughout the country and world.

Learning Technologies and the Educational Mission

The fifth century B.C. Greek author-adventurer Herodotus of Hallicarnasus introduced what has come to be considered the first secular narrative of Western civilization with the assertion that significant events of his age should "not in time be forgotten nor things great and wonderful." Based on this mission nine books emerged on pivotal events in ancient history, as well as about topics ranging from Egyptian mummification to the amber trade routes of Eastern Europe. The question of how Herodotus determined which topics were significant enough to merit attention in his "researches" is one of central importance to educators in any age. The issue reminds us of Herbert Spencer's timeless query that opened this work, "What knowledge is of most worth?" Herodotus's extensive travelogue-commentaries were not intended to advance this discussion. However, a contemporary living across the Aegean Sea in Athens, Socrates, based his teaching upon a belief that intellectual and moral improvement was the chief aim of learning. This improvement would arise as individuals affirmed virtue, justice, and piety in their personal life. Yet Socrates argued that these values could not be taught through formal didactic instruction. Rather, he believed they arose from a kind of illative process by exemplars in filial devotion and public service.

One of Socrates' most prominent students, Isocrates, advocated a formal pedagogy of rhetoric and other practical skills to prepare students for success in life. In some respects, these contrasting perspectives anticipate the academic vs. vocational debate that

Journeys
Book Report

"I think there is a lot we can learn from this story about how hatred based on ignorance can have terrible results. The diseases and violence endured by the native peoples resulted in conditions that continue to the present day. When Brennan found that skull and started thinking about what it must have been like to be killed at his age I thought...."

Lisa Moran,
8th grade

The Fremonts

"Altogether life seemed very bright and full of happy possibilities as we entered the Golden Gate. [But] we found a bleak and meagre frontispiece to our Book of Fate. There were then some three or four regularly built houses in San Francisco, representing the Hudson Bay and the Russian hide business; the rest were canvas and blanket tents."

Jessie Fremont, 1849

frames many educational decisions presently. The advent of learning technologies offers the prospect of delivering education in the context of more fully merging this duality in ways that will affirm their value for every individual. The mission of the Journeys of Discovery curriculum in the twenty-first century is what has long characterized a comprehensive education: the attainment of personal excellence. The mind's boundless capacity to acquire and apply knowledge for private and public benefit represents an inspiring basis for the mission of any student and teacher. Through carefully planned instructional experiences, cyberworld learning moves seemlessly into real-world applications to both build basic skill proficiencies and expand intellectual horizons. Students can actively participate in the democratic process by using communication technologies to research public issues, formulate position papers and action plans, and communicate their opinions to pub-

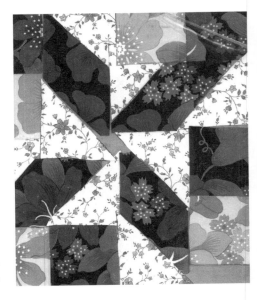

Pioneer Quilt Patterns,
wrapping paper

lic officials. Investigations of the natural world enable any instructional setting to become a laboratory where data can be collected locally or from anywhere on the globe and beyond, to build measurement skills and formulate and test hypotheses in accordance with the scientific method.

As writing is among the clearest expressions of higher order thinking, such undertakings in all subjects take students on research, journaling, and creative writing quests every bit as engaging as Herodotus' exploits throughout the ancient Mediterranean. In pursuit of this mission, learning technologies combined with interdisciplinary curricula like Journeys of Discovery dynamically provide the basis of direction, means, and community that can prepare a new generation of citizens for the opportunities and challenges of a new age.

"When I awoke in the forest, strange beings that resembled humans surrounded me. For some reason I was not afraid so I tried to make them understand where I was from. I decided to point to the sky and show them where Earth was located but the constellations all looked different. So I decided to stick to something I knew like baseball...."

Michelle Samuels, 7th grade

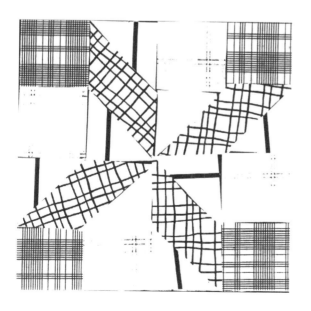

Conclusion

Sidebars:
The Campaigns of Theodore, and
Franklin & Eleanor Roosevelt

T. ROOSEVELT

"I was fortunate enough in having a father whom I have always been able to regard as an ideal man. It sounds a little cant..., but he really did combine the strength and courage and will and energy of the strongest man with tenderness and purity."

Theodore Roosevelt, 1900

Meaningful comparisons between the past and the present are difficult to make, and they are not even necessarily useful. Nostalgic reflections on a Golden Age of teaching and learning actually take us back to a time when only a favored few went to school for any serious amount of time. Today nearly everyone goes to school for many years.

The real difference between the educational past and the present is that today it really matters whether schools are effective, whereas in the past it probably did not because most people would make their livings in ways that did not depend on formal schooling. Less than a century ago, even less than that, the majority of people in the developed countries lived on farms and made their living from the soil. Now farmers account for less than two percent of the American and Western European population, even though the farms are more productive than they have ever been.

In the 20th century a great transformation took place from agriculture to industry, and the dominant mode of earning a livelihood became factory work. The average American and European in the 20th century was a factory or mill worker. The plain truth is that neither traditional farming nor factory work demand skills that you learn in school. Anyone with common sense could do those jobs, especially factory work which is essentially unskilled labor and semi-skilled at best. But by the year 2010, between five and ten percent of the population of the developed countries will be factory workers. The dominant mode of earning a living will be, and perhaps already is, information processing of one kind or another. The difference between information processing and farming or industrial work is that it does indeed demand school-related skills. We will probably be more productive industrially than we are now, but far fewer people will earn their livings as factory workers.

Thus we are in the midst of yet another great transformation. This time the change is from the Industrial Age to the Information Age. Just as the average nineteenth century citizen was a farmer, and the average twentieth century citizen was a factory worker, the average twenty-first century citizen will be an information processor. This means that the vast majority of people will be working in the service sector of the economy. Even farming and industry will employ more people in information processing than in tilling the soil and assembly line work. Already in the automobile industry, more people are employed in sales, insurance, advertising, design, and management than in the actual product assembly.

What can schools do to prepare young people to live in an information age? What transformations will schools and teachers have to make in order to become part of the solution rather than part of the problem? At the present time there is considerable reason to think that schools represent a major stumbling block in our attempts to make the transition from an industrial to an information society. This is not to say that our public schools are without good intentions; they are, in fact, citadels of good intentions, and within their walls are to be found some of the most good-hearted, hard-working people in all of society.

If the schools are willing to participate in the transformation from industrial to information society, they can be more than merely helpful, they can lead the way, something schools have never done before. Be warned, however, that the schools that will emerge and prosper in an information age may be so radically different from schools as we know them today that they will be outside our present sensibilities of what school is and ought to be.

First of all, there is an age-old controversy about the nature of schools and the sense of propriety that people have over how they should be run. Rather than having us get mired down in the complexities of this problem, let us simplify this division by noting that on one hand there is what we can call the "traditional" or "separate subjects" group, while on the other hand there is the "experiential" or "interdisciplinary" group. If we were to think of

"There were no schools in many places back in those days so young people spent much of their time learning about the world and traditions from their parents and elders. My grandfather has taught me much about the value of working hard and the importance of taking care of the land. Life was not easy for the pioneers because survival depended both on personal effort and cooperation with your neighbors."

Brent Repp, 7th grade

the labels as umbrellas then they are fairly large umbrellas capable of sheltering some range of differences under each.

Without question, schools have been, and continue to be, dominated over the years by the first group. The latter group, however, dates back at least to Socrates (who genuinely believed that a student had to learn for himself and that a teacher could at best merely facilitate the process) but has never been taken seriously by the majority of people. Generally speaking the experiential approach has at best functioned as an alternative approach to schooling. It is instructive to examine the characteristics of the two approaches to school. Their hallmarks, studied carefully, reveal deep and abiding differences.

On the one hand, the traditional point of view is based on an assumption that there exists a known and generally accepted body of content and skills that can be articulated with respect to scope and sequence, and that such information can be reasonably delivered by teachers to students in group settings over a period of years. Further, it is assumed that "experts" should develop the necessary curriculum materials, primarily in the form of textbooks and workbooks. The classroom teacher's job is to mete out, monitor, and measure the learning. Thus the teacher serves as a purveyor of the "scientifically" designed curriculum. Written work, tests, academic grades (even in nonacademic subjects), and promotion from one

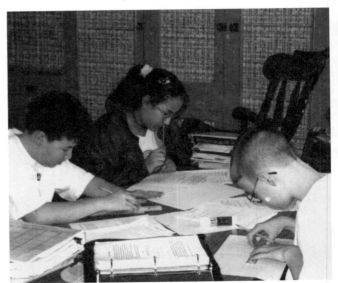

Classroom Research

level to the next are integral components of the curriculum. Instruction is generally aimed at whole groups, either grade level or ability, and it is taken for granted that all students within a group should proceed at the same pace in spite of the fact that we know that people learn at different rates. The content of the curriculum is basically derived from the traditional academic disciplines tempered by concessions to pressing societal needs. In lower grades, courses such as reading, language arts, social studies, and science are found. These broader based courses gradually give way to more focused offerings such as English, history, physics, etc. Courses such as driver education, drug refusal skills, and word processing are offered as "life skills" because the school setting seems to be the most reasonable place to teach them. Such a curriculum, with slight variations (for example, we have dropped Latin and typing and added Spanish and word processing) has been offered by the public schools for decades. This curricular approach is standardized, centralized, and synchronized, and represents an industrial model of schooling.

On the other hand, the experiential approach is based less on teaching and more on learning. The learner, rather than the teacher and the standardized curricular materials, becomes the focus. Ideas, not skills, are the working capital of this curriculum. The ancient doctrine of interest is invoked, and students are invited to

"Words to Live By"
There is no "I" in team.
Winners never quit, and quitters never win.
When the going gets tough, the tough get going.
Failure to prepare is preparing to fail.
Luck is when preparation meets opportunity.

Spenser Behrens, 6th grade

Student Cartographers

"No patent remedy can be devised for the solution of the industrial world's grave problems; but we may rest assured that they can be solved at all only if we bring to the solution certain old-time virtues, and if we strive to keep out some of the most familiar and most undesirable of the traits to which mankind has owed untold suffering throughout the ages."

Theodore Roosevelt, 1897

pursue their own ideas about what they want to learn. The teacher's job is to support and make possible the exploration of ideas by students. More than that, the teacher is responsible for creating the kind of physical, social, and intellectual environment that makes it possible for learners to become active explorers. Thus in fact the teacher's role becomes more challenging and complex. Textbooks and workbooks play a greatly diminished role. The reading of "real" books (biographies, novels, etc.) is encouraged. The fact that not all the students in a group have "covered" the same pages in a text is perceived as a strength, not a weakness, because this is not a centralized, standardized curricular approach.

Integration of subject matter, particularly with emphasis on thematic learning, is integral to this approach. Student-to-student interaction is encouraged in the form of cooperative investigations, discussions, and the sharing of work. Whereas in the old curricular approach, we did everything we could to keep students away from each other, now we are inviting them to talk to each other, to work together, and to share, not compete, for ideas. Problem-solving projects with their inherent syntactic complexities are focused on real-world outcomes. An example of this is the group of Canadian middle school students who mounted a successful campaign, complete with abundant research, to remove chlorofluorocarbon-containing styrofoam cups from use in their school district and in the British Columbia ferry system.

Thus the curriculum becomes localized, decentralized, and less predictably patterned. Little rote learning is encouraged, and students are expected to search for meaning, patterns, and relationships in the course of their studies. True intellectual rigor is demanded of students, but on their own terms, at their own pace, and in a variety of ways of demonstrating that learning is indeed taking place. Assessment is less standardized even though students who experience an exploratory curriculum generally do as well or better than their traditionally schooled counterparts. In conclusion, what we are describing here is a philosophy of curriculum that places emphasis on learning and learners and not on the predetermined material to be covered.

Perhaps a question would be helpful to determine where one stands with respect to these two conceptions of curricular reality. Recently a mathematician, Professor Alexander Abian, proposed that we blow up the moon. He reasoned that in so doing we would release the Earth from its 23 1/2 degree tilt from the perpendicular, setting it upright and creating a planet-wide springlike climate for the Earth. What do you think of his idea? Without getting all the specifics of your response, let me say that you probably have experiential tendencies if your response was one of openness. If your response was something along the lines of "it's a bad idea," or "we shouldn't even consider it," then you probably have other tendencies. The point is that almost every new idea, whether ultimately proved "workable," "useful," or "worthwhile," probably started out as an outrageous suggestion. What we are really talking about here is an *attitude toward learning and knowledge*, one of openness, tentativeness, and willingness to entertain the seemingly outrageous.

This is the profile of the learner that we so desperately need to cultivate in an information age. Consider these insights offered by Dwayne Huebner: "The problem, of course, is that schools and other institutions of education are not places of knowing, but places of knowledge. Knowledge is the fallout from the knowing process. Knowledge is separated from life. It stands by itself, removed from the vitality and dynamics of life, from the spirit. It becomes part of life only when it is brought once again into the knowing process of an individual. Until then it is dead. ...If the student is brought into the deadness of inert knowledge, the student is also deadened, alienated from the vitality that co-creates the worlds of self and others. By enlivening knowledge, the student is also empowered. To enliven knowledge is to accept it with doubt and to place it back into the eternal cycle of openness, love, and hope."

Heubner's observations invite us to consider the possibilities, to be open, to replace certainty with hope, and to invest ourselves wholly in the knowledge seeking enterprise. This can happen only when learners are allowed to explore, to choose the avenues of

Journeys Journal Entry

D: *Mom, why do I have to go to school today?*

L: *Oh, it's your choice so I guess you can stay home.*

(17 years later)

D: *We need cheeseburgers at table seven!*

Narrator: *I would just like to give you a word of advice: If you don't get into the habit of working hard as a kid, you can look forward to a life of minimum wage jobs. Work to achieve something because it won't come any other way.*

Derek Miller and Litney Leifer, 6th grade

T. ROOSEVELT

exploration, and to arrive at their own conclusions. The human spirit is endowed with the desire to learn, to know, to care, and to share. What is so often missing is the school-sanctioned opportunity to be truly free to learn.

Where the Process Begins

For the transformation to be meaningful you must be willing to accept the idea that a teacher must first be a learner. Your ability to model the excitement of learning to your students will be the key. The writer Charles Jones has noted that five years from now each of us will be nearly the same as we are today except for two things: the books we read and the people we get close to. Teachers ought to often remind themselves and their students of this thought.

Educational research indicates that the motivation to learn new ideas is more than anything else, the result of prior learning. In other words, the more you have learned, the more you are desirous and capable of learning. Therefore, teachers themselves must continue to seek new knowledge, and they must encourage their students to read, write, and investigate as much as possible. But this alone is not sufficient. School at its best is a socially contrived experience, and teachers should capitalize on that idea. Coopera-

White House Cardboard Model Project

tive work, student-to-student interaction, and the development of friendships must be part of the goal structure for learning in an information age. The students who will emerge from our schools best equipped to contribute to the quality of their own lives and to society will be those who have learned how to learn and who are eager and able to work with others in solving problems. Learning subject matter alone is not sufficient. We have seen altogether too many examples of high-achieving loners.

The following is an example of what happens when a lesson is well planned and carefully delivered, but where the motivation and affiliation factors are absent. An educational researcher at the University of Chicago, Mihaly Csikszentmihalyi, offered the sobering results of his research on what pupils are thinking about during class time. High school students were equipped with a device that prompted them to write down what they were thinking about at various time intervals. Teachers, meanwhile, were asked to note what they thought occupied their students' minds. While teachers assumed that students were pondering the subject matter during a lecture, only two pupils in one class studying the Mongol invasion of China, for example, were actually found to be thinking about China. One was daydreaming about a local Chinese restaurant and the other was pondering the long hair-

"Hi, I am reporting live from the White House which is the official home of the President of the United States. This beautiful residence was designed as an eighteenth century Englishman's country house. Although damaged by the British in 1814, it was rebuilt and extended by 1818. It would be cool to be the president's kid so you could play tag here in this mammoth house except if you accidently ran into a congressman."

Justin Quinton, 6th grade

The White House,
Kristi Curtis,
6th grade

T. ROOSEVELT

"There is a homely old adage which runs, 'Speak softly and carry a big stick; you will go far.' If the American nation will speak softly and yet build and keep at a pitch of the highest training a thoroughly efficient navy, the Monroe Doctrine will go far."

Theodore Roosevelt, 1903

style common to Asian men of that period!

Practical Steps

Finally, here are several practical steps that schools and teachers can take to facilitate this transition. These steps will work only if teachers are serious about bringing about a fundamental transformation in the ways in which we think about teaching and learning, and indeed the ways in which we think about the purposes of school.

1. *Meaningful Interaction.* For too many students, school has very little real meaning. This is true not only for low achievers but for many high achievers as well. Students are given work to do simply because it is part of the curriculum. They are required to complete assignments in order to be able to complete future assignments. Often students are given little or no choice about the work they are expected to do. In the first century AD, the Roman educator Quintilian introduced the "doctrine of interest." He boldly suggested that not all schoolwork should be contrived ahead of time for students, but that they, students, should be able to study the thing that interests them most. He wrote about the individual differences to be found among students, and he suggested that it would be profitable for teachers to study their students in order to find out what they wanted to learn. Centuries later, this thought was echoed by Jean Rousseau who suggested that a teacher's first duty was to get to know his students better, because, as he said, "you surely do not know them."

Given the assumption of an intelligent, caring, well prepared teacher, the key to meaningful learning is the relationship between teacher and student. A recent study showed that most adolescents say that very few (less than 10 percent) of the teachers they had in school had any meaningful effect on their lives. Those few teachers who did have a meaningful effect on the lives of their students were invariably teachers whom the students felt cared personally for those students they taught. Thus meaning comes not from carefully prepared lectures or from worksheets prepared by educational experts, but from shared encounters between teacher and student. When teachers take time to listen to their students, wonderful things begin to happen. Meaningful relationships develop; students begin to want to learn on their own.

2. *Make Connections.* In a recent research study, ten and eleven-year old students were given the opportunity to become involved in a class project of their own choosing. The class was asked to decide on something they would manufacture and sell to other students. They chose for their project to make simple denim-covered folders that other students could use to keep their papers. They manufactured, advertised, and sold their product. Each day the students worked on the project, dividing the labor among themselves. Many problems arose along the way, and the students had to solve them democratically. Each day, the teacher would spend a few minutes reviewing their work and discussing with them the economic ideas related to what they were doing. She explained such concepts as "supply and demand," "division of labor," and "human and material resources." The students would also read about and discuss these ideas as they related to their project.

In a comparison classroom, students studied a textbook on economics. They studied the same concepts that the project students studied. The difference was that the students in the comparison class studied economics as typical abstract schoolwork. At the conclusion of the study, students in both classrooms were tested on their knowledge of economics. The project students achieved much higher scores than did the comparison class. The reasons for the differences in achievement were clear: the project students were able to connect the economic ideas to their personal experience. Thus the ideas had meaning. For the students in the comparison group, it went "in one ear and out the other."

One other thing that emerged from this study is worth noting. The students in the project class worked together, talked together, decided together, etc. As a result, they reported that they made meaningful friendships with one another. A girl who had recently

Journeys
Editorial

Dear Editor,
I think it is wrong that we have free trade with China when they are putting people in prison because of their political or religious beliefs. Not very many years ago college students who were protesting the situation in the center of Beijing were killed by government forces and just this last year Buddhist temples in Tibet were invaded and monks forced to leave...."

Brooke Reynolds,
8th grade

F.D. ROOSEVELT

"In the course of the last four months it has been made probable through the work of Joliot in France, as well as Fermi and Szilard in America—that it may be possible to set up a nuclear reaction in a large mass of uranium, by which vast amounts of power and large quantities of new radium-like elements, would be generated."

Albert Einstein to Franklin Roosevelt, 1939

enrolled in the school was assigned to the project class. She had no friends. Life in school was painful and difficult for her. The teachers said that she was a good student but that she was very lonely and withdrawn. In the project class she quickly became involved with other students because the students needed to work together. She made several good friends and became a happier person. The students in the comparison classroom were so busy studying their worksheets that they had little or no time for meaningful relationships to develop, either with one another or with the teacher. Therefore, we as teachers desperately need to search for ways to bring about connections between students' experiences and interests and the academic skills and concepts that we want them to learn.

3. *Stop the Conveyor Belt.* Students who have experienced success in school experiences will be predictably eager to learn more. Students who have experienced failure will predictably become discouraged. They lose their motivation to learn. They fall behind in their studies and lose their desire to attend school. Their teachers become impatient with them. In time they come to dislike academic learning and anything associated with it. The key to motivation is to realize that almost all students can be successful achievers. Unfortunately, teachers often equate the rate at which a student grasps an idea or skill with the level of understanding. But this is wrong thinking on the part of the teacher. It is a proven fact

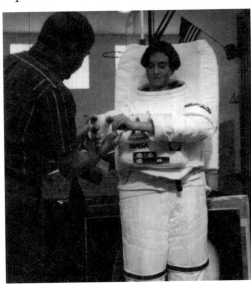

Young Astronaut Presentations

that speed of learning is not the same thing as depth of learning. In fact, some people who learn more slowly are able to learn in greater depth. Some people who learn quickly are not necessarily ultimately better learners than their slower counterparts. Centuries ago, the Greek writer Aesop told the tale of the tortoise and the hare in which he made this very point: the race is not necessarily to the swift; slow but sure wins many races.

When we erroneously equate rate of learning with ability to learn, we leave many students behind who were perfectly capable of learning whatever it was that we were trying to teach. This has disastrous effects because once you fall behind it becomes increasingly difficult to catch up, and your motivation toward further learning is destroyed. Therefore, as teachers you must consider the possibility that perhaps some students are slower to learn because they see the complexities inherent in the material, and are taking a deliberate approach to the subject. But whatever the reason, patience is called for. People who are not patient should not be teachers. Teachers must patiently sow the good seed if they wish to reap a bountiful, worthwhile harvest.

4. *Teach Less.* Jean Rousseau wrote that we should teach less, and teach it well. This is a powerful insight. Rather than cover so much material in your teaching, identify the few key ideas that you know are the most important and teach them in depth. Visit

Supplies and Materials for the Journeys Classroom

- Multiple copies of *National Geographic Magazine, Smithsonian, Discover* or similar magazines organized by year that can be used for student research on a variety of topics. Back issues of *Geographic* are often obtainable from used book stores or subscribers in the community.
- Tourist brochures and booklets on regions of the world under study. These informative and colorful resources are often surplused by tour companies several times each year and are ideal for research, art projects, and other purposes.
- Equipment for scientific observation and recording including low-power binocular microscopes with illumination lamps and scales for weighing.
- A good working relationship with the school and local public librarians. Their help is invaluable for obtaining books, videos, and other materials for student and teacher use during the journey.

Jo Petersen, Ocean Beach Public Schools, Ilwaco, Washington

"I think it is interesting that some of the most important American scientists of the twentieth century came to this country because of problems in their homeland. The ones who were most responsible for the development of nuclear technology, for example, include Einstein who was from Germany, Enrico Fermi who was Italian, Leo Szilard of Hungary,....."

Maria Sanchez, 7th grade

them and revisit them using meaningful examples and appropriate applications. If an idea is truly worth learning, it should be complex enough to be examined from a variety of points of view so that it becomes clearer and clearer to those who must learn it.

The great Russian novelist Nikolai Vasilievich Gogol wrote a story called *The Overcoat* in which a poor bureaucrat saves his money in order to have a tailor make him a handsome winter coat. The coat becomes the most important thing in the man's life. Every day he stops by the tailor's shop to see how his coat is coming along. At night the man dreams of the coat and how fine he will look in it. When the garment is at last finished the man dons it proudly and steps out into the winter night only to be beaten and robbed of his new coat. The story can be read for the writer's style as well as for a glimpse of life in nineteenth century Russia. It is also a study of shattered dreams. But the point is that the story is worth taking one's time over. Each time it is read new thoughts emerge. This is the case with anything worthwhile. The parables of Jesus, Aesop, and others have been told for centuries because of the truth they contain. Their modern-day applications are endless. They can be studied over and over because of the insights they provide. Mathematical ideas such as the Pythagorean Theorem or the fixed ratio between the circumference and diameter of a circle ($C=\pi D$) have symmetry and beauty worthy of reflection and application.

Perhaps the best way to teach less and teach it well is as follows:

1. Be sure that you can identify the key ideas for whatever you set out to teach.

2. Be sure that you do not try to cover too much material at one time.

3. Be sure that you allow your students time to talk with one another and reflect on the key ideas of an assignment.

4. Be sure that you give your students opportunities to apply the ideas they learn in a variety of ways which emphasize spiritual, practical, aesthetic, and intellectual implications.

5. Think less about teaching and more about learning.

It is useful to observe children at play if you wish to make the transition from teaching to learning. They will show how to do it. I'm not talking about adult-supervised soccer or baseball for children. That is the opposite of play. Those are regimented activities that are planned and arbitrated by adults, thereby allowing none of the complexities of mental, moral, and spiritual insight that are possible in true play. For example, in an adult-supervised game involving ten- and eleven-year old boys and girls an argument broke out over some obscure rule. The children were told to sit down and stay out of the way while the adults quarreled among themselves thus effectively depriving the children of the opportunity to attempt to resolve a conflict that at the moment had real meaning. These children were not players in the most meaningful sense of the term; they were, rather, game pieces in an adult activity.

When young children play together in the dirt or in a mud puddle, they spend much of their time discussing ideas and creating imaginary worlds. They invent activities, rules, roles, and so on. To the best of our knowledge, no pedagogue has written up the rules or provided worksheets and testing procedures for playing in dirt and mud. Children playing video games are interesting to watch. Especially fascinating are their debriefing conversations in which they reflect with each other on the strategies and skills needed to achieve various levels of the game to the point of mastery. Guidebooks are written for the video games, and often a child will devour one searching for ways to master a particular game. But whether we are considering mud puddles or video games, the point is the same, namely that no one teaches this stuff. You just get involved in the enterprise, do it to the best of your ability, learn from each other, and read on your own.

These same procedures are at work in classrooms where teachers themselves are excited about learning new things and where they have provided an environment filled with interesting things to do and learn about. Learning takes on a playful, informal tone, and a surprising amount gets done. The teacher moves around

Journeys
Journal
Entry

"I admire Dr. Albert Schweitzer for leaving a comfortable life in Germany in the 1920s and going to central Africa to help people who did not have doctors. He was famous before leaving Europe since he had devoted many years to the study of science, music, and religion. He received the Nobel Peace Prize...."

*Cameron Adams,
7th grade*

the room talking to students, mediating their questions, and providing a forum in which group activities and discussions can take place in addition to the individualized work that students carry out. Students in these environments tend to read more, talk more with their fellow students and teachers, and in general exhibit a greater love of learning than do their counterparts in more traditional classrooms. Why? Because they have made the important transition from being taught to becoming learners.

If we are to make a successful transition into an information age of schooling, teachers must be willing to reconsider their fundamental role. We must be willing to abandon the idea that teaching is telling. We must be willing to embrace the concept of the exploration of ideas by teachers and students working together. We must set aside our thoughts of school based on a production-oriented, industrial model. We must be willing to cross the frontier from teaching to learning.

The Judeo-Christian legacy places emphasis upon the unique, God-given characteristics and talents of every individual and Eastern traditions value social obligations and collective responsibility. Both contribute to the democratic process, which is based on principles of equality, openness, and human rights. This heritage for humantiy has the potential to offer hope that justice will be served in meeting the needs of the next generation.

To be a teacher represents the highest calling. The American historian Henry Adams wrote that teachers affect eternity; they never know where their influence will stop. Every encounter we have with a young person is part of the cumulative affect that shapes a life. A good teacher is not merely knowledgeable about subject matter; a good teacher is a model for life. This must be our calling.

Appendices

A Journeys of Discovery
Lesson Sequence

Table of Contents

Study Guide 1.4 – **A Private Secretary**

The United States
Capitol, 1800

Heading—

38° N. Latitude, 77° W. Longitude.

Problem Solving—

When Lewis wrote from Pittsburgh, how far was he from Washington City (D.C.)?

Editing—

I did not receive your letter untill two late friday by that days mail. (4) [Lewis to Jefferson, March 10, 1801]

Discussing—

___ 1. Lewis accepted Jefferson's offer to become his private secretary.
___ 2. Lewis was honored to serve his country.
___ 3. "Nothing endures but personal qualities—nothing."
       (Walt Whitman)

Constructing—

Thomas Jefferson wrote thousands of letters in his lifetime. Write a letter asking someone to work for you. Explain the job and describe the qualities needed in the person you wish to hire.

Fort Pitt (Pittsburgh) was a frontier outpost located on the Ohio River. Do some research about life in these forts of early America, and report your findings. Build a model or draw sketches of a fort.

Connecting—

Meriwether Lewis was an infant when the American Revolution began. Read the book *Sam the Minuteman* by Nathaniel Benchley to help you understand the young nation in which Lewis lived.

William Seale, *The President's House: A History,* Washington, D.C.: NGS and the White House Historical Association, (1986).

Sidetripping—

The **White House** in Washington, D. C., has been the official residence of the President since 1800. Every chief executive since Thomas Jefferson has lived there. It was burned by the British in 1814, was restored in the 1820s, and rennovated in 1902. The interior was completely redesigned between 1948 and 1952 to match the Georgian style of the original Architect, James Hoban.

Defining—

secretary:

character:

render:

confidence:

receipt:

cipher:

Washington, D. C.

While Jefferson used the term "secretary" *for this position, he generally wrote his own letters even when in office and sought rather to have a special assistant to organize meetings, his schedule, and serve as a personal representative.*

relinquish: *From the Latin prefix re-, behind, + linquere, to leave; meaning to abandon or release.*

1.4 A Private Secretary

—Jefferson to Lewis

Washington, February, 23, 1801

Dear Sir

The appointment to the Presidency of the U.S. has rendered it necessary for me to have a private secretary, and in selecting one I have thought it important to respect not only his capacity to aid in the private concerns of the household, but also to contribute to the mass of information which it is interesting for the administration to acquire. Your knowledge of the Western country, of the army and of all its interest & relations has rendered it desirable for public as well as private purposes that you should be engaged in that office. In point of profit it has little to offer; the salary being only 500. D. which would scarcely be more than an equivalent for your pay & rations, which you would be obliged to relinquish while withdrawn from active service, but retaining your rank & right to rise.

But it would be an easier office, would make you know & be known to characters of influence in the affairs of our country, and give you the advantage of their wisdom. You would of course save also the expense of subsistence & lodging as you would be one of my family. If these or any other views which your own reflections may suggest should present the office of my private secretary as worthy of acceptance you will make me happy in accepting it. It has been solicited by several, who will have no answer till I hear from you. Should you accept, it would be necessary that you should wind up whatever affairs you are engaged in as expeditiously as your own & the public interest will admit, & adjourn to this place and that immediately on receipt of this you inform me by letter of your determination.

It would also be necessary that you wait on General Wilkinson & obtain his approbation, & his aid in making such arrangements as may render your absence as little injurious to the service as may be. I write to him on this subject. Accept assurances of the esteem of Dear Sir your friend & servant.

Th. Jefferson

—*[Lewis to Jefferson]*

Pittsburg, March 10, 1801

Dear Sir,

Not until too late on Friday last to answer by that day's mail did I receive your much esteemed favor of the 23rd Ult. In it you have thought proper so far to honor me with your confidence, as to express a wish that I should accept the office, nor were further motives necessary to induce my compliance, than that you Sir should conceive that in the discharge of the duties of that office, I could be serviceable to my country, or useful to yourself Permit me here, sir, to do further justice to my feelings by expressing the lively sensibility with which I received this mark of your confidence and esteem.

I did not reach this place on my return from Detroit until late on the night of the 5th instant, five days after the departure of General Wilkinson. My report therefore on the subject of your letter was immediately made to Colonel Hamtramck, the commanding officer at this place. Not a moment has been lost in making the necessary arrangements in order to get forward to the City of Washington with all possible despatch. Rest assured I shall not relax in my exertions. Receive I pray you, sir, the most undisassembled assurance of the attachment and friendship of your most obedient, & very humble servant,

Meriwether Lewis

∴

The faintly glowing Pleiades cluster *of the seven star sisters are located just below the bright red star Aldebaran (al-DEB-ah-ran) in Taurus. To the Cherokee Indians of Virgina and the Southeast, the seven stars are the "The Boys" who began a dance in defiance of their mothers' discipline. They were taken up into the sky for this disobedience except for one who fell deep within the earth. From this spot grew the yellow pine which then spread throughout the South.*

Ult. *is the abbreviation for ultimo which means in or of the preceding month.*

James Wilkinson *(1757-1825) was commanding general of the U.S. Army in 1801 and later served as governor of the Territory of Louisiana.*

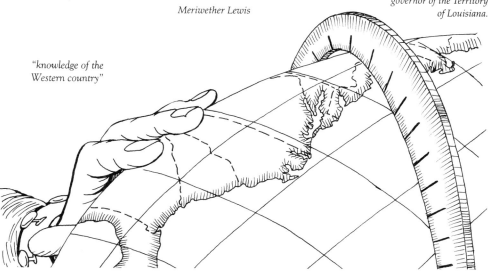

"knowledge of the Western country"

1.4 – Onondaga Reservation, Onondaga and Oneida Tribes

Nedrow, New York
(Area: 7,300 acres)

The semilegendary Chief Hiawatha of the Onondaga founded the Iroquois Confederacy in the 16th century despite initial opposition from many tribal leaders of the Five Nations. His eloquence and wisdom convinced others that the advantages of unity would greatly benefit their peoples' future. In the first formal proposal for a union of the American colonies, Benjamin Franklin cited the the Iroquois Confederacy as a model at the 1754 Albany Convention. The Onondaga chief is the hero of Longfellow's famous poem.

The Iroquois Tribes of New York and Pennsylvania were members of the Six Nations of the Iroquois League, which was founded by the peace prophet Dekanawida and his disciple Hiawatha. The league was originally formed by five tribes; the related Tuscarora not joining until 1716 when they moved to the area from the Carolinas. Although organized for mutual defense, the league became a powerful Indian empire, the force behind much of the intertribal pressures in the Midwest and West. As the central nation in the founding of the confederacy, the Onondaga are the "Keepers of the Fire." The league's decline after two centuries of prominence was largely the result of involvement in disputes between French, English, and American colonists. Most of the members of the league supported the British in the French and Indian War and Revolutionary War. This alliance gave Britain the advantage over France, but proved damaging to the league's negotiating base following the American victory.

The Indian name of the Iroquois described a people dwelling in longhouses, the characteristic structures of Iroquois bark assembly halls, council houses, and composite family dwellings. Several families, usually related through the female line, lived in a longhouse. All property was owned and inherited by the women. Although they were the military masters of most of the northeastern United States, the Iroquois preferred to use diplomacy in settling differences. The are most widely acclaimed, however, for their moral caliber and organizational effectiveness. Today the reservation functions and looks like any other community with the people still maintaining the ancient ceremonies of their ancestors. An annual field day is open to non-Indians and is called the Green Corn Dance.

The Onondaga, most conservative of the Iroquois Tribes, are organized around the Longhouse religion. The chiefs who govern the Onondaga Reservation are chosen in the traditional way and are chiefs for life. As required by tradition, the chief of the entire Iroquois Nation must be an Onondaga. He is the Tadodaho, and only he can summon the Six Nation Council. The Onondaga Reservation remains the capital of the confederacy and the Onondaga Tribe maintains that, as a foreign nation, it has a special relationship to both the federal and state government.

Wild Rice and Turkey Soup

3 lbs. turkey meat	1/2 tsp. thyme	1 bay leaf	2 small chopped carrots
4 cups of cooked wild rice	1/2 tsp. parsley	1/3 chopped onion	salt and pepper to taste

Put turkey meat into a pot with 8 cups of water and boil. Add the rest of the ingredients and let simmer for about one and a half hours. Add the wild rice and continue to simmer for another half-hour.

Journey Update 1.4 – **George Catlin and the National Museum**

Catlin's "Gallery Unique" on display in Paris, 1845

The Smithsonian Institution was established by Congress in 1846 to serve as a national research center, museum, and library devoted to founder James Smithson's goal of increasing knowledge and sharing it with the public. Smithson was an Englishman who never visited America but had a distinguished career in Europe in chemistry and mineralogy. He willed his fortune to the United States to establish the institution named in his honor. Today it consists of a dozen separate museums, building some seventy-five million artifacts, specimens, photographs, works of art, and other objects owned by the United States government. These collections are stored and displayed in the National Museum of History and Technology which contains the flag that is the subject of the national anthem: "Star-Spangled Banner," the National Air and Space Museum, the National Gallery of Art, and the National Zoological park

The National Collection of Fine Arts contains 590 works by George Catlin who devoted his life to painting scenes of North American Indian life. Catlin's offer to sell his entire collection of paintings to the Smithsonian in 1849 for $65,000 was refused by Congress but most of them were acquired in 1879 through private sponsors. Today they comprise the Catlin Gallery of the National Collection. Other important collections of Catlin's works are held by the American Museum of Natural History in New York City and the Gilcrease Institute of American history and Art in Tulsa, Oklahoma.

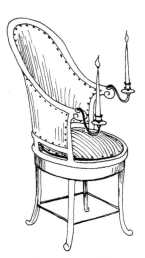

Night-writing swivel chair,
invented by Jefferson

17th century
Swept-Hilt Rapier

Social Studies 1.1 – Thomas Jefferson's America

I Rise With the Sun

"Whether I retire to bed early or late, I rise with the sun." That, according to Thomas Jefferson, is how a typical day in his life began. For over fifty years the sun never caught him in bed. He would rise as soon as he could read the hands on the clock in his bedroom, all year round. The first thing he did was measure and record the temperature. Around four o'clock each afternoon he would repeat the measurement. Jefferson also made a practice of recording the direction and speed of the wind and daily amounts of precipitation. He checked a weathervane frequently to read the wind, cross-checking the reading with a compass dial. Thomas Jefferson noted migrations of birds and the appearance of flowers throughout his life, in Virginia, in Philadelphia, in Washington D.C., even in France. Wherever he would go he carried with him a variety of portable instruments for making observations and measurements, objects like scales, drawing instruments, a thermometer, a level, and even a globe. He also carried a small ivory notebook on which he could write in pencil. Later he would copy the information in ink into books he kept on his garden, farms, finances, and other concerns. He then erased the writing in the ivory notebook so he could use it again.

Jefferson shared his records with others, and hoped to create a national database of meteorological information. Clearly, when Thomas Jefferson called upon Lewis and Clark to explore the land beyond the western border of their new nation, he had some definite measurements in mind. This nation, the United States of America, contained a great diversity of inhabitants. Some had descended from immigrants who had arrived about two hundred years before the new nation was born. Some were Native American with ancestors who had walked the land for untold generations past. Some, like Jefferson, had been born of immigrant fathers at the precise time in history when the United States was established. What they all had in common by 1803 was a stake in the future closely linked to westward expansion into uncharted territory. The intent of President Jefferson was to make that territory known, and known in great detail. So Lewis and Clark left the security of the familiar Eastern American culture and set out to explore the unknown, not unlike their ancestors had done two hundred years earlier.

New Faces in the Neighborhood

Having been born a Virginian, Thomas Jefferson was mindful of the important role the Virginia Colony had in the story of America. The first permanent English-speaking settlement in America was established in Jamestown, Virginia in 1607. The name "Virginia," now one of the United States of America, was then a name applied to a colony in honor of the "Virgin Queen of England," Elizabeth I. The Virginia Colony covered almost the

Literature 1.2.1 – The Catskill Mountains

by Washington Irving

The Catskill, or Cat River Mountains, derived their name in the time of the Dutch domination from the catamounts by which they were infested. With the bear, the wolf, and the deer, they are still to be found in some of their most difficult recesses. The interior of these mountains is in the highest degree wild and romantic. Here are rocky precipices mantled with primeval forests, deep gorges walled in by beetling cliffs, with torrents tumbling as it were from the sky, and savage glens rarely trodden excepting by the hunter. With all this internal rudeness, the aspect of these mountains towards the Hudson at times is eminently bland and beautiful, sloping down into a country softened by cultivation and bearing much of the rich character of Italian scenery about the skirts of the Appennines.

The Catskills form an advance post of the great Appalachian system of mountains which sweeps through the interior of our continent, from the southwest to northwest, from Alabama to the extremity of Maine, for nearly fourteen hundred miles. They belt the whole of our original confederacy and rival our great system of lakes in extent and grandeur. These vast ramifications comprise a number of parallel chains and lateral groups such as the Alleghenies, the Green Mountains of Vermont, and the White Mountains of New Hampshire. In many of these vast ranges, nature still reigns in indomitable wildness. Their rocky ridges and rugged clefts and defiles teem with magnificent vegetation.

Here are locked up mighty forests that have never been invaded by the axe; deep umbregeous valleys where the virgin soil has never been outraged by the plow; bright streams flowing in untasked idleness, unburdened by commerce, unchecked by the mill-dam. The mountain zone is, in fact, the great poetical region of our country; resisting like the tribes that once inhabited it the taming hand of cultivation and maintaining a hallowed ground for fancy and the muses.

The Catskill Mountains maintain all the internal wildness of the labyrinth of mountains with which they are connected. Their detatched position, overlooking a wide lowland region with the majestic Hudson rolling through it, has given them a distinct character and rendered them at all times a rallying-point for romance and fable. To me they have ever been the fairy

Washington Irving
(1783-1859) may be best known for his popular stories about legendary events along the Hudson River Valley like "Rip Van Winkle" and the "Legend of Sleepy Hollow". Irving was born in New York and grew up hearing tales about the early Dutch settlers of the region. He collected these and other stories in New England and traveled to Europe to do the same during the same years Lewis and Clark were crossing America. Many of his New England stories were first published in The Sketch Book of Geoffrey Crayon in 1820 which made him famous both in American and Europe.

He was fascinated by the journals of Lewis and Clark and decided to make his own journey to the American frontier in present Missouri, Kansas, and Oklahoma in 1832. This led to his book A Tour of the Prairies (1832) and later works based on the accounts of early fur traders for Astoria (1836) and The Adventures of Captain Bonneville (1837).

Literature 1.2.2 – The Thunder Power of Rumbling Wings

by M.R. Harrington

Imagine *that you magicially traded places with an Indian warrior who rose from one the great moundbuilder earth tombs in which he had so long rested. The author of this story, former director of the Heye Museum of the American Indian in New York, weaves such a tale which is set in the homeland of the Lenape or Delaware Indians who inhabited an area stretching from Delaware northward into southeastern New York.*

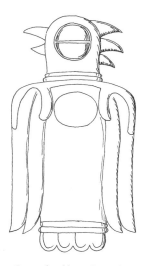

Copper headdress plaque from an Ohio mound

When I came to myself I could see nothing, but I knew it was raining steadily. I could hear the drops patter on the leaves. I could feel them on my body. On my body? I felt my chest, it was bare and wet, my arms likewise. I felt at my waist; it was belted and in front hung something like an apron. My legs? I found them encased is long stockings of some sort, reaching nearly to the hips. As I bent over to feel of my feet, something brushed against my cheek, something hard and cold, yet light and almost clinging. I put up my hand and felt. It seemed to be a string or rather loop of little beads.

Puzzled, I started to run my fingers through my hair—a favorite habit of mine, and I found that I almost had none! That is none to speak of—it was very short indeed, almost as if shaven, except for a bristly crest which ran from front to back over the top of my head, and ended in a queue in the back. I looked about me; it was still raining and a brisk wind stirred the tree tops. I seemed to be in a strange, wild country for, although I could look off over a valley, my eye met no sign of man except a distant blur of smoke, rising apparently from among the trees. I looked behind me. There stood a great tree, its wood showing white, its bark practically stripped off, while broken branches littered the ground. It had been struck by lightning.

I pulled the knife from its sheath. It was of stone—argillite—not purple from age, but black, fresh-looking, sharp. And I found a little decorated pipe of clay, and with it some damp, shriveled leaves which must have been some sort of tobacco. I could not avoid the conclusion. I was somehow transported back into prehistoric times. If this were true, I must have some weapons, I thought, and soon I found them—a five foot, straight bow, lying beneath the broken branches that had fallen from the lightning-blasted tree, and a buckskin quiver. I pulled out the arrows; their points were of flint. The carcass of a deer lay also among the fallen branches, evidently a victim of the bow. I noticed I was feeling hungry so I slung my quiver, picked up my bow, and after a moment's hesitation, shouldered the deer and started down the hill toward the smoke.

Mathematics 1.3 – Timelines & Measurement

1. Work with a partner to create a timeline for the first 50 years of Jefferson's life. Use centimeters to represent years. Be sure to allow room to extend the timeline. Select significant events from his life and place them along the timeline at the appropriate year. Underneath your year scale, fill in the age scale.

   Create your own timeline. Select 5-6 significant events from your life and fill them in along your timeline. Predict the future—determine when you will graduate from high school and/or college, start a career, etc.

Extensions:

   Add some significant historical events to your timeline and Jefferson's timeline.

2. Using the map of Virginia and the District of Columbia you created in Travelogue Reading 1.1, draw a centimeter grid over the map. Use the grid to approximate the area of the District of Columbia in square centimeters. Use an atlas and other references to find the actual area of the District of Columbia. Determine the scale of your map. (Hint: How much area does 1 square represent on your map?)

3. Use the timeline you created for Thomas Jefferson's life. Add in significant dates for Meriwether Lewis. Below Jefferson's age scale, create an age scale for Lewis.

4. If George Catlin had sold his collection of 590 paintings to the Smithsonian in 1849 for $65,000, determine the average price per painting that the Congress would have paid. What percentage of all the artifacts in the Smithsonian does the George Catlin collection represent?

5. Work with a partner to construct a measuring device to calculate distances. Use your device to find the distance from your classroom to a fixed point such as the school fence or a tree. What are some of the strengths and weaknesses of this measuring device? What do you deed to know to use this measuring device?

Career Connection:

Space Pysicists

President Jefferson *asked Lewis and Clark to investigate the vast natural and physical realm of the North American continent. They also took measurements of stars and planets and sought to understand Native interpretations of various constellations. Modern space scientists expanded knowledge of magnetic and electric fields, radiation and streams of electrified particles, or plasma, and other phenomena of the relationship between the earth and the solar system. Space physicists have launched satellites to increase scientific knowledge of the earth's atmosphere and magnetosphere, and to gain practical benefit by monitoring the effects of space radiation on electronic equipment. They also are involved in chemical release experiments designed to aid other scientists studying the processes by which neutral gases become ionized, or electronically charged. Using a comprehensive array of ground and air instruments, including tracking radars, telemetry systems, and other equipment, space physicists study the clouds prior to, during release, and just after each chemical release.*

Sciences 1.4 – **The Science of Geology**

by Charles Lyell

Sir Charles Lyell
(1797-1875) is one of the most important figures in the history of modern geology. Following the ideas of his fellow Briton James Hutton, Lyell challenged the most popular and widely accepted beliefs of earth, its history, and its future. He traveled extensively over years of study, cultivating his beliefs through discovery. Though not widely accepted in his own day, Lyell's theory revolutionized the modern view of earth's changes and influenced many scientists, including Charles Darwin, in forming theories of their own.

During the time of Lyell's youth, the influence of James Hutton, considered the "father of modern geology" who died the same year Lyell was born, was still being felt around the scientific world. Hutton introduced a theory far different from the widely accepted "catastrophism," which held that only major catastrophes could change the basic forma-tion of the earth's surface. Hutton's theory was called "uniformitarianism," and held that natural processes such as volcanic activity, sedimentation, and erosion had been operating in the same way and at the same rate since the beginning of time. In short, its theory was "the present is the key to the past."

Geology is the science which investigates the successive changes that have taken place in the organic and inorganic kingdoms of nature. It inquires into the causes of these changes, and the influence which they have exerted in modifying the surface and external structure of our planet. By these researches into the state of the earth and its inhabitants at former periods, we acquire a more perfect knowledge of its present condition, and more comprehensive views concerning the laws now governing its animate and inanimate productions.

When we study history, we obtain a more profound insight into human nature, by instituting a comparison between the present and former states of society. We trace the long series of events which have gradually led to the actual posture of affairs. By connecting effects with their causes, we are enabled to classify and retain in the memory a multitude of complicated relations—the carious peculiarities of national character—the different degrees of moral and intellectual refinement, and numerous other circumstances, which, without historical associations, there would be uninteresting or imperfectly understood. As the present condition of nations is the result of many previous changes, some extremely remote, and other recent, some gradual, others sudden and violent. So the state of the natural world is the result of a long succession of events. If we would enlarge our experience of the present economy of nature, we must investigate the effects of her operations in former epochs.

We often discover with surprise, on looking back into the chronicles of nations, how the fortune of some battle has influenced the fate of millions of our contemporaries, when it has long been forgotten by the mass of the population. With this remote event we may find inseparable connections to the geographical boundaries of a great state, the language now spoken by the inhabitants, their peculiar manners, laws, and the religious opinions. But far more astonishing and unexpected are the connections brought to light, when we carry back our researches into the history of nature.

The form of a coast, the configuration of the interior of a country, the existence and extent of lakes, valleys, and mountains, can often be traced to the former prevalence of earthquakes and volcanoes in regions which have long been undisturbed. To these remote convulsions the present fertility of some districts, the sterile character of others, the elevation of land above the sea, the climate, and various peculiarities, may be distinctly referred. On the other hand, many distinguishing features of the surface may often be ascribed to the operation, at a remote era, of slow and tranquil causes— to the gradual deposition of sediment in a lake or in the ocean, or to the prolific increase of corals.

Fine Arts 1.5.1 – **Journal Binding**

Background: Of all the explorations in the United States history, probably the most talked about, studied, and dramatized journey was the Journey of Discovery made by Meriwether Lewis and William Clark. The most likely reason for this is because we have their invaluable journals. Lewis and Clark and Patrick Gass wrote extensively during their trip. There have been books, films and re-enactments of their struggles because we have such complete knowledge of the saga. Lewis and Clark were admonished by President Jefferson to make observations and these were to be made with "great pains and accuracy, to be entered distinctly and intelligibly." The dramatic story of Lewis, Clark, Sacagawea, and the men of the Corps of Discovery has been well and beautifully recorded.

The oldest examples of books are on stone. We don't know for certain how soon people began to make what we would consider a book; that is, something written of considerable length meant for circulation which requires being portable. Probably the most direct ancestors of the modern book are the papyrus scrolls of Egypt, which date back 2500 years. The first Chinese books were probably done as early as 1300 B.C. It is the codex that is the modern form of the book. Instead of having pages fastened together to extend in a strip, the codex was made from folded leaves bound on one side, or in some cases at the top. Codex and roll books existed at the same time, but there are references to codex books in the First Century B.C. Vellum and parchment are made from animal skins. Early printing and illustrations were done with wooden blocks but it was for the German printers to cast metal type, develop an oil based ink, and construct the printing press. Today the publication of books is essential to our civilization.

Bookbinding began with the codex form. (The word codex is from the Latin word *caudex* which means tree trunk. Some early book bindings were made of wood.) The first really beautiful book bindings were of decorated leather. Later wooden boards were covered with tooled leather and fitted with metal clasps, gilt decoration, gold tooling, and inlaid patterns. Early books were considered works of art. Modern books are produced and bound by machinery.

George Catlin *(1796-1872)*
was a Pennsylvanian born artist and traveler. While hunting alone in the woods at the age of ten, he met an Oneida Indian named Great Warrior, whom he befriended and from whom he learned about Native American life. Later that year, Great Warrior was murdered near the Catlin's farm and the tragedy left a deep impression on the boy. As a young man, Catlin was elected to the Pennsylvania Academy of Art in Philadelphia, where he met a delegation of Indians. After this meeting, Catlin vowed, "Nothing short of the loss of my life shall prevent me from visiting their country, and of becoming their historian." To this end, he traveled extensively across America and met William Clark in St. Louis in 1830, where the famous frontiersman had served as Governor of the Missouri Territory since 1813. Clark became Catlin's patron and he painted the Governor's portrait and that of dozens of the prominent Indian leaders and scenes of village life. Three hundred of these priceless images appeared in his book Letters and Notes on the Manners, Customs, and Condition of the North American Indians (1841).

Sacred Indian Peace Pipes

State Note A.1 – **The Boundaries of Virginia**

Thomas Jefferson
from Notes on the State of Virginia

In a brief paragraph
*describe the boundaries of your
state. How does its location
influence trade with other
states and nations?*

Virginia is bounded on the East by the Atlantic, on the north by a line of latitude, crossing the eastern shore through Watkin's Point, being about 37° 57′ North Latitude. From there a straight line goes to Cinquac, near the mouth of the Potomac; thence by the Potomac, which is common to Virginia and Maryland, to the first fountain of its northern branch. From there a meridian line passes through that fountain till it intersects a line running east and west, in latitude 39° 43′ which divides Maryland from Pennsylvania and which was marked by Messrs. Mason and Dixon. That line continues westwardly by the completion of five degrees of longitude from the eastern boundary of Pennsylvania, in the same latitude, and then by a meridian line to the Ohio.

Virginia is bordered on the west side by the Ohio and Mississippi, to latitude 36° 30′ North and on the south by the line of latitude last mentioned. By measurements through nearly the whole of this last line, and supplying the unmeasured parts from good data, the Atlantic and Mississippi are found in this latitude to be 758 miles distant, equal to 13° 38′ of longitude, reckoning 55 miles and 3,144 feet to the degree. Our latitude, taken between this and Mason and Dixon's line, is 3° 13′ or equal to 223.3 miles, supposing a degree of a great circle to be 69 miles, 864 feet, as computed by Cassini.

© Mountain Light Media

B. The Shoshoni – **Grandfather of Nations**

A Native American play, edited by Arden S. Johnson

Sources

James Athearn Jones, *Tales of an Indian Camp* (London, Henry Colburn and Richard Bentley, 1830), Ella E. Clark, *Indian Legends From the Northern Rockies* (Norman, Oklahoma: University of Oklahoma Press, 1966), and Emily Peone, oral histories with Richard Scheuerman (Nespelem, Washington, 1987).

Background

Native American groups had drama in their lives but did not have theatre. They expressed themselves through art but in storytelling, mask making, songs, dancing, and painting rather than putting on what we would call a play. The storytellers became very dramatic and proficient in passing the culture to the next generation. Tribal ways and history, ritualistic procedures and the origin of the sacred stories were usually told on winter evenings. Fables and narratives gave moral and ethical instruction. Some stories and legends satisfied normal curiosity. It was the duty of the elders to hand down the traditions to the younger generations. The Shoshones believed that they could only tell the traditional stories in the winter time or snowy months.

It is suggested that in preparation for this pageant the students be informed of the Native American oral traditions. It should be explained how native peoples passed down legends and stories which became great dramatic events stimulating the imagination of the people. The stories, told under the dark skies of night, while seated in the flickering light of small fires with the dark forests looming close by must have taken on great importance. This performance could be presented as a masked story or a puppet play. Either way the pre-performance work entails important preparation.

Before undertaking any performance of these stories, the students should also be given many mask making/puppet making opportunities, and be asked to give suggestions on how the performance as written here could be performed for an audience that would simulate story-telling and stimulate the imagination of the audience. Young people often have marvelous ideas of how something should "look." Masks can be elaborate or simple. Three-dimensional, many-colored, cut paper masks, somewhat replicating carved wooden masks, can be mounted on sticks and this makes it easy for students to have many roles. More elaborate papier mache masks can be made as part of this lesson, or even a combination of several kinds of masks can be part of the lesson. Shadow puppets mounted on sticks are also a possibility.

As the narrative is read with students, ask the class for help in the preparation. For example, there is a very alarming scene when a rattlesnake comes to life on the prairie. The rattlesnake is really a mighty and wise man in disguise. One suggestion would be a series of masks each becoming larger and more frightening in visage. However, students know what scares them,

Cast

Rattlesnake

Storyteller

Red Arrow

Coyote

Chief of the Strangers

Marmot

Spy

Crane Person

Grandmother

Children (3-5)

Sunflower

Crane People (3-5)

Bird Woman

Whistling Swan

Sisters (3)

Maiden

Novel Guide C.1 – The Ghosts of Stony Clove

he Ghosts of Stony Clove is set in the early 1800's. Asher and Ginny are young teens that have grown up together. Because of the superstitions that were rampant in the day, Ginny was one of this half Indian's only friends.

Asher's parents, believing that they were leaving him in good care, left him with a family when he was a young boy. Asher became nothing but an extra farm hand for the Stone family. Ginny's father had died, leaving her family to be raised only by her mother.

One night, at a harvest festival, the two young teens decide to explore Stony Clove. This area had long been the topic of ghost stories and hauntings for several generations. This evening's adventures would change both of these young people of the rest of their lives.

The journey begins...

Before you begin to read *The Ghosts of Stony Clove*, look at the table of context page. The author gives you two dates, two months apart. In the first, short chapter of the book, the author indicates that what you are going to read is a first person account of what many believe is a legend. Think about what defines a legend. Discuss with other students some legends that you may know. Are there any common threads that run through these legends. As you read *The Ghosts of Stony Clove*, look for these common elements.

Charting the course...

Fear is more than a feeling. It is a disease that can rule people's lives. One of this stories underlying currents is fear. Fear in the unknown. Fear in strange people. Fear in secrets revealed.

Before reading *The Ghosts of Stony Clove*, thumb through the pages and look for reoccurring people's names that you can see are the main characters of the story. On a separate sheet of paper list five of these names in a column going down the left side of the paper. Next, make two more columns across the top of the page. Label the first one "Fear" ands the second column, "How this fear is conquered."

As you read the book, note the fear that the named character displays and how the author resolves their fears.

On the back of your chart, note words that are used in the story that are new or unfamiliar to you. Try and learn their meaning from the context clues that are given or look them up in a dictionary. Save this list to use at the end of the story.

Journey's end...

At the end of *The Ghosts of Stony Clove*, the author includes an article written in the late 1800's about people and places similar to what are related in the book. After reading this section, what are your feelings about the story?

D.1 – Wood River Camp (December, 1803 – May, 1804)

HO Scale Model Cutout Pattern (1"=9'), Designed by Robert Saindon

Wood River Camp was located in Illinois along Wood River directly across from the Missouri's confluence with the Mississippi River. It took sixteen days to construct, and here the Corps of Discovery spent the winter of 1803-04 preparing for their journey up the Missouri. The original site has been eroded away due to the shifting of the river's current, but a monument nearby commemorates this historic place.

Directions

Fort model assembly requires only a scissors, dull knife for scoring, and glue. Round toothpicks may be used to cover walls and roofs to simulate logs.

1. With a dull knife, lightly score all dash lines -- -- -- -- -- -- . **2.** Cut out all five cabins.

3. Along the dashed lines fold each cabin into shape and glue the tabs in order of their numbers. Leave the unnumbered tabs without glue until you reach direction number five.

4. The chimneys are found on pages V.63.2 and V.63.4. Cut out and fold into shape, apply glue to the tabs, and attach to the cabins.

5. Apply glue to the bottoms of the cabins and attach them to their proper places on the Wood River ground plan found below.

6. Cut out the fences on page V.63.4, attach them to the ground plan.

7. After each fort has been constructed, cut out the facings on pages V.63.3 and V.63.4 and glue them into their proper places.

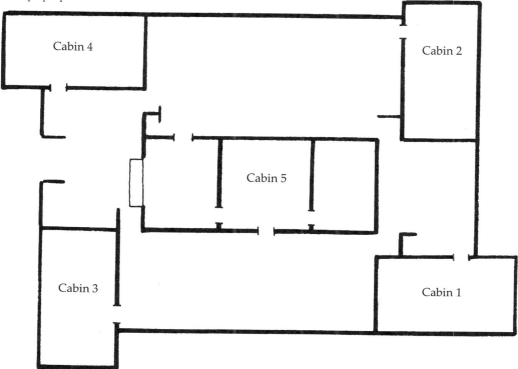

Wood River Camp Cabins and Chimneys

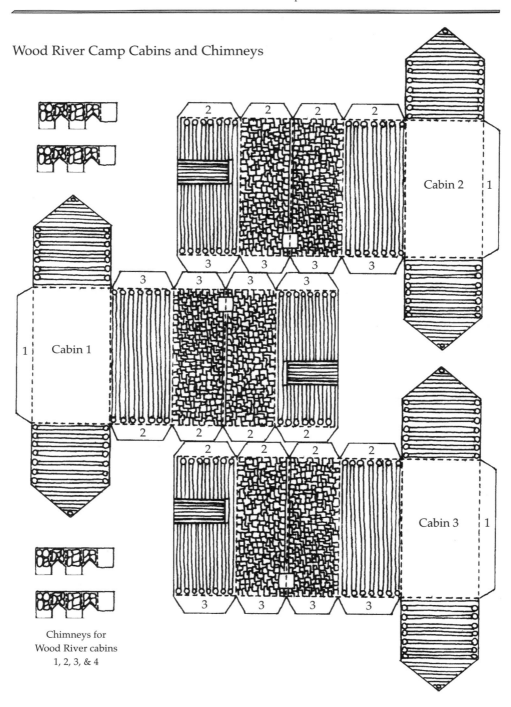

Chimneys for
Wood River cabins
1, 2, 3, & 4

References and Suggested Readings

The Mountain Light School Community
Spring, 1921

Interdisciplinary Instruction

Barzun, Jacques. *Begin Here: The Forgotten Conditions of Teaching and Learning*. Chicago: The University of Chicago Press, 1991.

Beane, James A. *Curriculum Integration: Designing the Core of Democratic Education.* New York: Teachers College, Columbia University, 1997.

Brooks, Jacqueline. *In Search of Understanding: The Case for Constructivist Classrooms*. Alexandria, Virginia: Association for Supervision and Curriculum Development, 1993.

Ellis, Arthur L. and Carol Stuen. *The Interdisciplinary Curriculum*. Larchmont, New York: Eye on Education, 1998.

Gardner, Howard. *The Unschooled Mind: How Children Think and How Schools Should Teach*. Cambridge, Massachusetts: Perseus Publishing, 1993.

Jacobs, Heidi. *Interdisciplinary Curriculum: Design and Implementation*. Alexandria, Virginia: Association for Supervision and Curriculum Development, 1989.

General Exploration

Anderson, J. R. L. *The Ulysses Factor: The Exploring Instinct in Man*. New York: Harcourt Brace Jovanovich, Inc., 1970.

Asimov, Isaac. *Exploring the Earth & the Cosmos*. New York: Crown Publishers, Inc., 1982.

Boorstin, Daniel J. *The Discoverers*. New York: Random House, 1983.

Hall, Stephen S. *Mapping the Next Millennium*. New York: Random House, 1992.

Leed, Eric. *Shores of Discovery: How Expeditionaries Have Constructed the World*. New York: BasicBooks, 1995.

Maddox, John. *What Remains to be Discovered: Mapping the Secrets of the Universe, the Origins of Life, and the Future of the Human Race*. New York: The Free Press, 1998.

Morison, Samuel Eliot. *The Great Explorers: The European Discovery of America*. New York: Oxford University Press, 1978.

Obregon, Mauricio. *Argonauts to Astronauts: An Unconventional History of Discovery*. San Francisco: Harper & Row, Publishers, 1980.

The Annals of Herodotus, Alexander & Pliny: Classical World Journeys of Discovery

Carpenter, Rhys. *Beyond the Pillars of Heracles: The Classical World Seen Through the Eyes of Its Discoverers*. New York: Delacorte Press, 1966.

Glover, T. R. *Herodotus*. Berkeley, California: The University of California Press, 1924.

Hamilton, Edith. *The Greek Way/The Roman Way*. New York: Bonanza Books, 1986.

Meijer, Fik. *A History of Seafaring in the Classical World*. New York: St. Martin's Press, 1986.

Sarton, George. *A History of Science: Hellenistic Science and Culture in the Last Three Centuries*. Cambridge, Massachusetts: Harvard University Press, 1959.

Selincourt, Aubrey de. *The World of Herodotus*. Boston: Little, Brown and Company, 1962.

The Sagas of Leif Ericsson and Early Feudal Kings: Northern European Journeys of Discovery

Brøndsted, Johannes. *The Vikings*. Great Britain: Penguin Books, 1976.

Bullough, Donald. *The Age of Charlemagne*. Elek Books, 1965.

Holand, Hjalmar R. *Norse Discoveries & Explorations in America 982-1362: Leif Erikson to the Kensington Stone*. New York: Dover Publications, Inc., 1969.

Mapp, Alf J. Jr. *The Golden Dragon: Alfred the Great and His Times*. La Salle, Illinois: The Open Court Publishing Company, 1974.

Mowat, Farley. *Westviking: The Ancient Norse in Greenland and North America*. Boston: Little, Brown and Company, 1965.

Eleanor of Aquitaine and the Crusade of the Kings: Medieval European Journeys of Discovery

Kelly, Amy. *Eleanor of Aguitaine and the Four Kings*. Cambridge, Massachusetts: Harvard University Press, 1950.

Lacroix, Paul. *Science & Literature in the Middle Ages and the Renaissance*. New York: Frederick Ungar Publishing Co., 1964.

Matthews, John. *King Arthur and the Grail Quest*. London: Brockhampton Press, 1998.

Ohler, Norbert. *The Medieval Traveller*. United Kingdom: The Boydell Press, 1989.

Payne, Robert. *The Dream and the Tomb: A History of the Crusades*. New York: Stein and Day Publishers, 1984.

The Travels of Marco Polo and Ibn Battuta: Asian and African Journeys of Discovery

Dunn, Ross E. *The Adventures of Ibn Battuta: A Muslim Traveler of the 14th Century*. Los Angeles: The University of California Press, 1986.

Hart, Henry H. *Venetian Adventurer: The Life and Times of Marco Polo*. Palo Alto, California: Stanford University Press, 1942.

Olschki, Leonardo. *Marco Polo's Asia*. Los Angeles: The University of California Press, 1960.

Rossabi, Morris. *Kublai Khan: His Life and Times*. Los Angeles: The University of California Press, 1988.

Severin, Timothy. *The Oriental Adventure: Explorers of the East*. Boston: Little, Brown and Company, 1976.

The Exploits of Columbus and the Conquistadors: New World Journeys of Discovery

Fitzhugh, William W. *Cultures in Contact*. Washington D. C.: Smithsonian, 1985.

Morison, Samuel Eliot. *Admiral of the Ocean Sea: A Life of Christopher Columbus*. Boston: Little, Brown and Company, 1991.

Sale, Kirkpatrick. *The Conquest of Paradise: Christopher Columbus and the Columbian Legacy*. New York: Alfred A. Knopf, Inc., 1990.

Elizabeth I and the Explorations of Drake and Raleigh: English Seafaring Journeys of Discovery

Chapman, Walker. *The Golden Dream: Seekers of El Dorado*. Kansas City: The Bobbs-Merrill Company, Inc., 1967.

Nicholl, Charles. *The Creature in the Map: A Journey to El Dorado*. New York: William Morrow and Company, Inc., 1995.

Rowse, A. L. *The Elizabethans and America*. New York: Harper & Brothers, 1959.

Sugden, John. *Sir Francis Drake*. New York: Henry Holt and Company, 1990.

The Voyages of James Cook and Alexander Mackenzie: Pacific Journeys of Discovery

Beaglehole, J. C. *The Exploration of the Pacific, Third Edition*. Palo Alto, California: Stanford University Press, 1968.

Fisher, Robin and Hugh Johnston. *Captain James Cook and His Times*. Seattle: University of Washington Press, 1979.

Hough, Richard. *Captain James Cook: A Biography*. New York: W. W. Norton & Company, 1995.

Howse, Derek. *Background to Discovery: Pacific Exploration from Dampier to Cook*. Berkeley, California: University of California Press, 1990.

O'Brian, Patrick. *Joseph Banks: A Life*. Boston: David R. Godine, Publisher, 1993.

The Narratives of Smith, Hutchison and Bradford: Colonial Journeys of Discovery

Emerson, Everett. *Captain John Smith: Revised Edition*. New York: Twayne Publishers, 1993.

Franklin, Wayne. *Discoverers, Explorers, Settlers: The Diligent Writers of Early America*. Chicago: University of Chicago Press, 1979.

Lemay, J. A. Leo, *The American Dream of Captain John Smith*. Charlottesville: University Press of Virginia, 1991.

Notson, Adelia W. and Robert C. Notson, ed., *Stepping Stones: The Pilgrims' Own Story*. Portland, Oregon: Binford & Mort Publishing, 1987.

The Chronicles of Crèvecoeur, Franklin and Bartram: Early American Journeys of Discovery

Campbell, James. *Recovering Benjamin Franklin*. Chicago: Open Court Publishing Company, 1999.

Philbrick, Thomas. *St. John de Crèvecoeur*. New York: Twayne Publishers, 1970.

Slaughter, Thomas P. *The Natures of John and William Bartram*. New York: Alfred A. Knopf, Inc., 1996.

The Expeditions of Lewis & Clark and Zebulon Pike: North American Journeys of Discovery

Botkin, Daniel B. *Our Natural History: The Lessons of Lewis and Clark*. New York: G. P. Putnam's Sons Publishers, 1995.

Dumbauld, Edward. *Thomas Jefferson, American Tourist*. Norman, Oklahoma: University of Oklahoma Press, 1976.

Furtwangler, Albert. *Acts of Discovery: Visions of America in the Lewis and Clark Journals*. Chicago: University of Illinois Press, 1993.

Hollon, W. Eugene. *The Lost Pathfinder: Zebulon Montgomery Pike*. Norman, Oklahoma: University of Oklahoma Press, 1969.

Jackson, Donald. *Thomas Jefferson & the Stony Mountains: Exploring the West from Monticello*. Chicago: University of Illinois Press, 1981.

The Adventures of John & Jessie Fremont and Kit Carson: Frontier American Journeys of Discovery

Egan, Ferol. *Fremont: Explorer for a Restless Nation*. Garden City, New York: Doubleday & Company, Inc., 1977.

Estergreen, N. Morgan. *Kit Carson: A Portrait in Courage*. Norman, Oklahoma: University of Oklahoma Press, 1993.

Goetzmann, William H. *Exploration and Empire: The Explorer and the Scientist in the Winning of the American West*. New York: Monticello Editions, 1993.

Herr, Pamela. *Jessie Benton Fremont: American Woman of the 19th Century*. New York: Franklin Watts, 1987.

Hine, Robert V. *In the Shadow of Fremont: Edward Kern and the Art of American Exploration, 1845-1860, Second Edition*. Norman, Oklahoma: University of Oklahoma Press, 1982.

The Campaigns of Theodore, Franklin and Eleanor Roosevelt: Modern American Journeys of Discovery

Collier, Peter. *The Roosevelts: An American Saga.* New York: Simon & Schuster, 1994.

Freedman, Russell. *Eleanor Roosevelt: A Life of Discovery.* Boston: Houghton Mifflin Company, 1997.

Meltzer, Milton. *Theodore Roosevelt and His America.* Danbury, Connecticut: Grolier Publishing, 1994.

Schlesinger, Arthur M., Jr. *The Age of Roosevelt, 4 vols.,* Boston: Houghton Mifflin Company, 1957.

Index

About the Authors

Arthur Ellis is professor of education and director of the International Center for Curriculum Studies at Seattle Pacific University. He is a former secondary school teacher and author of twelve books on issues in education. Dr. Ellis has been a consultant on various National Science Foundation curriculum projects and has lectured extensively in England, Russia, and China.

Richard Scheuerman is a middle level teacher and director of curriculum for St. John-Endicott Cooperative Schools in Washington State. He is the recipient of the Governor's Writers Award and Robert Gray Medal for contributions to education in the humanities and has been named an Outstanding Leader in Elementary and Secondary Education by the Association for Supervision and Curriculum Development.